Surviving Your First Year
at University

Surviving Your First Year at University

Catherine O'Connor with Liz Thomas

McGraw Hill

Open University Press

Open University Press
McGraw Hill
8th Floor, 338 Euston Road
London
England
NW1 3BH

email: enquiries@openup.co.uk
world wide web: www.openup.co.uk

First edition published 2021

Copyright © Open International Publishing Limited, 2021

All rights reserved. Except for the quotation of short passages for the purposes of criticism and review, no part of this publication may be reproduced, stored in a retrieval system, or transmitted, in any form or by any means, electronic, mechanical, photocopying, recording or otherwise, without the prior written permission of the publisher or a licence from the Copyright Licensing Agency Limited. Details of such licences (for reprographic reproduction) may be obtained from the Copyright Licensing Agency Ltd of Saffron House, 6–10 Kirby Street, London EC1N 8TS.

A catalogue record of this book is available from the British Library

ISBN-13: 9780335249596
ISBN-10: 0335249590
eISBN: 9780335249602

Library of Congress Cataloging-in-Publication Data
CIP data applied for

Typeset by Transforma Pvt. Ltd., Chennai, India

Fictitious names of companies, products, people, characters and/or data that may be used herein (in case studies or in examples) are not intended to represent any real individual, company, product or event.

Proviso: *The information contained in this book does not relate to any one university or programme of study but can be taken as a general guide to what to expect. It is the responsibility of the students attending to gain a knowledge and understanding of the practices, rules and regulations pertaining to their institution.*

Praise page

Going to University is an exciting time but it can also feel scary and overwhelming. This excellent guide helps demystify some of the technicalities, so students can easily navigate the system; more importantly it provides great advice on how to take full advantage of the many opportunities University life offers to develop personally as well as academically, and to achieve your full potential. Recommended reading for anyone keen to make the most of this brilliant life opportunity.
> Lynda Brady, Pro Vice Chancellor (Student Experience),
> Edge Hill University, UK

I believe this will appeal as a kind of A-Z of university life, as well as a guide to support students through their first year and beyond. ... It is clear the authors have considered the transition to university life from a range of perspectives, not just an academic one, which is particularly helpful for the challenges students face entering higher education.
> Christie Pritchard, Student Learning Manager,
> University of Plymouth, UK

The authors' commitment to the student experience, and the importance of a university environment that enables all students to reach their full potential shines through. This will be a vital guide for students embarking on this most important of transitions.
> Juliette Sargeant, Interim Director Library and Student
> Support Services, University of the Arts London, UK

In this accessible research and experience based book Catherine O'Connor and Liz Thomas offer established and new, helpful suggestions on how to not just survive but to thrive in their first year and throughout their time at University. This is essential reading for anyone studying or beginning to study in higher education.
> Gina Wisker, Head of Centre for Learning and Teaching,
> University of Brighton, UK

<u>Student Endorsements</u>

This book is a must read for everyone. There is something in it for everyone who wants to start university, just started or is already there. With this book the author created a holistic approach and provides multiple perspectives for all life circumstances during the life in university and beyond.
> Nils Lenoch, Student, Copenhagen Business Academy, Denmark

In this book Catherine O'Connor with Liz Thomas' shares an honest and direct message about life as you begin University and leave as a graduate. Scared that you won't fit in, that the course you choose may not be the right one, that you will not be getting a job afterwards? Well, most students including myself feel exactly like this when they begin University. This time is different because from this book you can learn all the tips and tricks on how to manoeuvre University life for the first time.

Fiona Nashie, Student, University of Westminster, UK

Contents

Foreword x

Introduction xii

PART I	STARTING YOUR UNIVERSITY JOURNEY	1
	Fears and expectations	2
	Starting the journey	2
	Living at home	5
	Living away from home	6
	How a university works	9
	Diversity	10
	Different systems	10
	The tutoring system	13
	Why students withdraw from courses	14
	Budgeting for your needs	17
	Handbooks	19
	Student toolkit	19
	Mature students	20
	Working part-time	21
	Concluding paragraphs	23
	Troubleshooting section	23
PART II	MAKING IT YOUR UNIVERSITY	26
	Freshers and pressures	26
	Structure of the academic year	27
	Delivery and assessment	28
	Academic challenges	29
	Handbooks	30
	Absences from university	32
	Communicating with your university	33
	Tutor system	34
	Class representatives	35
	Academic activities	36
	Examinations	45
	Grading system	46
	Independent study time	46
	University support services	47
	Drawing on your personal resources	52
	Concluding paragraphs	53
	Troubleshooting section	53
PART III	UNIVERSITY SKILLS	56
	Studying to get results	57
	Setting goals	57

	Managing time effectively	58
	Team working and learning	60
	Study groups	61
	Thinking critically and analytically	62
	Preparing for lectures	63
	Making the best use of notes	63
	Study skills and memory	64
	Listening skills	66
	Research skills	66
	Academic writing skills	67
	Essay writing	72
	Assessment	72
	Referencing and plagiarism	74
	Going digital	75
	Communication and presentation skills	76
	Concluding paragraphs	80
	Troubleshooting section	81
PART IV	**HEALTH, IDENTITY AND SOCIETY**	**83**
	Culture and diversity	84
	Gender and identity	85
	Sexual consent	85
	Travelling and studying abroad	86
	Looking after yourself	87
	Suicide	99
	Anxiety	99
	Substance use and abuse	100
	Developing resilience	100
	Seeking help	101
	Troubleshooting section	101
PART V	**LOOKING AHEAD**	**103**
	Section 1: Preparing for your second year	103
	Academic	104
	Social	104
	Making more friends	105
	Part-time jobs	106
	Internships	107
	Volunteering	108
	Work placements	109
	Preparing for graduate employment	110
	Section 2: Third year/fourth year and beyond	110
	University resources	112
	Job fairs	112
	Internships	113
	Graduate schemes	113
	Gap year	113
	Looking for work	114
	The future of work	120

Employability	120
Entrepreneurial spirit	121
Intrapreneurial spirit	121
The value of a university education	122
Postgraduate study	122
Lifelong learning	124
The gig economy	124
Global connectivity	125
Concluding paragraphs	126
Troubleshooting section	127
Selected Reading	129
Useful Links and Resources	131
Index	134

Foreword

If you were travelling to a new country you would invest in a guidebook to help you navigate the different cultural expectations. You would want a guidebook that provided accurate information about where you need to go to get the best experiences as well as advice and tips on what you need to do to make the most out of your trip. That guidebook would also point you in the direction of who locally you could ask for advice and assistance to ensure you enjoy your time there. Any good guidebook would also have information that, on first reading you may think will not be relevant to you, but as your journey progresses and unexpected challenges occur the guidebook, probably by now slightly tattered and well-worn, saves you with the exact piece of information you need for that moment. Surviving First Year is that handy companion.

When you first leave home to journey to another country you may consider yourself a tourist, but after months navigating your new surroundings you feel like a traveller but towards a year in one place you probably identify as a local as you are now culturally aware of how things work in the place you now call a home from home. This book is your guide to moving from nervous holiday-maker to innocent tourist to becoming a local, comfortable and confident in your new environment.

University is a bit like a different country with its labyrinth of departments and acronyms, myriad of rules and regulations and a whole new set of people alien to you. Just like travel university is exciting and full of promise and it brings a freedom away from traditional structures of home. This freedom means it is up to you to take advantage of the attractions and learning opportunities and Surviving First Year is a great guide to help you build the structure you will need to make the student experience your own.

Surviving First Year is a good title for however confident you are about attending university everyone has highs and lows in your first year as a student. This is normal. If you are ever struggling, or having a bad day, then it is vital you don't think, "is it just me?" It isn't. Going to university is a challenge and is not easy. Every single person starting something new needs time to settle in. Everyone requires information, advice and guidance to give them the best chance of surviving first year to thriving in subsequent academic years.

This thorough guide to success is a great resource for your journey and should be used as the 'pre-departure planning guide', the 'check-in guide so you can ensure you are covering all aspects of university' and the 'emergency, I'm not sure what to do/who to ask' guide. It can also be a reference for those at home wanting to know what your opportunities are and to help pinpoint support if required. The troubleshooting sections in the book are great for parents/carers to use to remind your student of the top tips.

The book provides practical advice for a successful transition into and first year at university, focusing on preparing students for changes in their lives, including the pitfalls encountered in university in the first year, what to expect, where to look for assistance and who to ask for help. On any university journey there will be different challenges and you will need to develop new skills to be successful. Your guide covers multiple topics; academic, social, financial and personal. As with any good travel guide a focus is on starting your journey, then making the experience yours with a whole section on the skills you need to achieve success. University, just like travelling, is an opportunity to discover you and who you really are and there is a section dedicated to this important activity. Finally, university is just part of your journey and looking ahead to career and next steps is important. While not everyone knows their exact destination, all good travel experiences produce surprising twists, knowing where you want your journey to take you helps focus in your next required steps.

Being successful in your degree is not just about academia and this book helps you to reflect on the skills you will need at university to become a successful student such as how to deal with the realities of the expectations placed on you. Important skills such as time management; goal setting; thinking critically and analytically and ways to improve academic writing skills are covered. As are the equally important skills of learning about your identity; looking after your physical and emotional and financial well-being and how to manage inter-personal relationships. The book has an important section on how to seek help and while asking for help may feel hard this book provides guidance on who to ask. Universities want you to reach your academic potential and know challenges arise, which is why all institutions provide extensive support services.

This is an important book to help you consider all aspects of university and provides you with expert advice and guidance to navigate your time there. Enjoy your journey.

Nic Streatfield
Head of Student Support and Wellbeing at University of East London
AMOSSHE – The Student Services Organisation Vice Chair
(Professional Development)

Introduction

Welcome to *Surviving Your First Year at University*, a practical guide full of insights and tips to help you make a smooth transition to university – and ultimately follow an easier path through and complete the journey at university. This guide is suitable for all students, British and international, entering undergraduate courses at university in England. Much of the advice will also be useful to students attending other higher-level institutions.

Approximately 2 million students participate in higher education in England today and 1.5 million of those are undergraduates.

Participating in study at this level brings you into a community of scholars and teachers which derives its meaning from the Latin translation *universitas magistrorum et scholarium*. On reading this book, you will get insights into how this community operates and tips on how to navigate the system in which it operates.

Surviving at university rests on your ability to ask questions; to find out how things work, what services are available to you and how you can use them; and to understand how to become a successful student and how to belong to a new community of learning.

Having spent many years working to get to this stage, you will benefit from gaining an early understanding about what this new experience will be like, what will be expected from you and ways to manage the transition effectively.

Over the course of the coming year, and indeed the following years, you will be faced with many challenges, and the information contained in this book might spare you from some of the many pitfalls which catch students off guard and negatively affect their progress both socially and academically at university.

The book is divided into five distinct parts, with a troubleshooting section at the end of each part addressing some *Frequently Asked Questions* which provide some tips for managing the way forward and on building employability skills. This section will also address concerns of international students attending English universities.

In the first part, we will look at the fears and expectations of students, how a university works, why research is important and the principal differences between the school and university education systems. It will also address the diverse population of the student body at university and look at ways to get used to your new environment, settling into new accommodation, managing finances and coping with the adjustment to the new system of learning. It will also look at living at home and away from home, and how to balance working part-time to support your studies.

In the second part, we look at how you make the university yours, from the pressures with Freshers, incorporating both the social and academic. We look at how you can make it your place of learning, getting down to the business of understanding the academic demands on your time. We also cover what student services are available to you and how to go about availing yourself of them. This part will also introduce you to the important and established tutoring support system at universities in England, together with an explanation of the many and varied interactions which might comprise a typical day in your life as a student.

In the third part, we look at the skills you will need at university to become a successful student: how to deal with the realities of the expectations placed on you. We look closely at managing time, setting goals, team working and learning, thinking critically and analytically, and ways to improve academic writing skills. Preparing for the examination process is also dealt with in this section together with communication and presentation skills, online engagement and digital skills.

Part IV deals with the issues surrounding health, identity and society which are paramount in taking control of all aspects of your life and your overall well-being. We look at culture and diversity, gender and identity, together with looking after your physical, mental, emotional and spiritual self. We also explore the area of interpersonal communication. The issues of suicide, substance abuse, sleep health and anxiety are also addressed. A series of exercises complements this part. Students are encouraged to complete these exercises which establish strengths and gaps in both personal and professional growth. We encourage you to set goals following the identification of these strengths and gaps, which in time helps you develop resilience, a skill which is key to dealing with the unexpected challenges that arise during the university experience and far beyond. University is not just about the academic experience. It's a preparation for another chapter in life's journey, an ever-changing world.

Part V, the final part of the book, moves past the first year, preparing you for your second-year experience and far beyond. Once you get through your first year, you will need to start thinking around the corner and looking for opportunities to enhance your learning and development opportunities but managing to bypass some of the typical pitfalls in this process.

This part will go further to addressing some of the challenges you may face in the third and fourth years and things to look out for on the way. It will look at internships, volunteering, taking a gap year, work placements and the growing adjustment of social and academic integration during the university years. It also looks at the future of work, the skills employers might be looking for and the different types of work in our world today, and how your academic achievements can adapt to fit into the future uncertainty of the work environment.

A selected reading list together with a useful links/resources section will complete the publication.

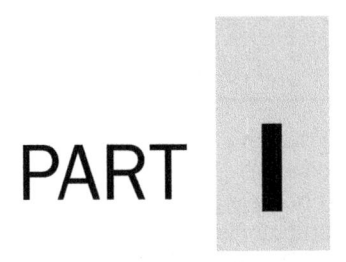

PART I
Starting Your University Journey

We will now look at how the university works and bring you to a greater understanding of what to expect, giving some insights into how you might begin your journey – incorporating discussion in the following specific areas:

- Fears and expectations
- Starting the journey
  - Arriving at university
  - Adapting socially
  - Making friends
  - The Students' Union
- Living at home
- Living away from home
  - Settling into accommodation
  - Homesickness
  - Some essential life skills
- How a university works
- Diversity
- Different systems
  - Changing relationships
  - Independent learning and critical thinking
- The tutoring system
- Why students withdraw from courses
- Budgeting for your needs
- Handbooks
- Student toolkit
- Mature students
- Working part-time

Fears and expectations

Many thoughts will be going through your mind at this time of great change.

Will I fit in? Will I be academically able for my course?

You may be one of the few students who has no concerns about either fitting in academically or socially, but many things will still niggle your mind as you start this new journey. Most students pass through this stage without too much complication and genuinely look forward to a positive and rewarding study experience. For many though it's not quite that straightforward. Mixed emotions will flood your mind. In this section, we can look towards alleviating a lot of the concerns you might have, which include:

- I'm afraid I won't fit in
- I don't want to be different
- I want to make new friends but I'm terrified that I'll end up alone
- I'm worried about moving away from my family and old friends
- I feel under financial pressure before I start
- I'm not sure that I will like this experience
- I don't want to make my old mistakes – I want to make a fresh start
- I don't know if I am academically ready
- I'm terrified of failing
- I want to branch out and meet new people

The first thing to remember is that all of these concerns are normal. You are not alone. Stand proud that you have reached this stage. We have all walked into a crowded room and felt a sense of panic and the wish to flee without explanation. If this happens to you, you will need to breathe deeply, hold your head high, remember why you are here and push yourself beyond your comfort zone. Once that initial fear passes, things will get a little easier. You have come from a school system where you were at the top of ladder and now you are back on the first step – but not for long.

Life at university is more than an academic experience. Your social development is equally important and making friends is an integral part of that development. Before we delve into the academic side, we will explore the social aspect of the university experience and how you can overcome some of those challenges.

Starting the journey

Up to this stage in your education, most of the major decisions you have taken have been shared with your parents, guardians, teachers or mentors. Indeed, many of these decisions may have been made for you. Now you have been catapulted into a very different place. Put simply, this means that you are about to take total ownership and responsibility for the next part of your academic journey in life. This is the key to making a success of the first-year experience, and research tells us that a good first-year experience at university is indicative of further success in the following years.

This time is about how you want to live your life. It's an opportunity to do things differently, to opt in or out of whatever you wish to engage in, at whatever time suits you and wherever that might take you. That self-management in itself sounds most attractive; however, it is this part of the experience that many students find the most difficult. Probably for the first time in your life, you have full control over how you wish to grow and develop in your new-found freedom. This is your destiny, and this book is written with exactly that in mind – giving you insights and tips to help you grow and develop on that journey, taking control and ownership on the way.

Arriving at university

The first few days will seem very strange. All universities put on special induction/orientation days for you which will take in familiarization with the geography of the campus, the libraries, the canteens, the various societies, the laboratories and much more. You will be given your timetable during this period and you will also be encouraged to get involved in the many activities which are especially designed for first-year students – commonly referred to as Freshers' week. Attendance during this induction/orientation process is key to settling into your new life, as you will meet so many new students who are also finding their feet in this time of transition.

This time is an opportunity to meet key academics, personal tutors and mentors. You will also be introduced to student ambassadors who, together with tutors and mentors, provide ongoing support during the first year.

Academic matters will be addressed, and you will be introduced to the handbooks relevant to your course of study.

Adapting socially

This point in your life is a most exciting time when you will have more freedom both academically and socially. No doubt you are looking forward to studying something new and exciting, doing what you want to do. However, university life is much more than an academic experience.

We all want to belong and feel part of a community, and starting university is no different in this regard. You will be worried about making friends, meeting new people and expanding your social circle. You may also feel guilty about leaving your old school friends behind and breaking ties with what has been so familiar to you for many years.

Taking steps into the unknown creates anxieties for many students in transition. These feelings are normal, but a lot of students find the new social scene overwhelming and meeting new people and making new friendships challenging.

You may feel that you are different to others starting out, and that in itself will make you feel uncomfortable. Take comfort from the fact that all new starts in life bring anxious periods, especially when you have to move out of your comfort zone and that secure canopy of school education.

Students generally find fitting in socially more difficult than fitting in academically. You have chosen your academic path in advance so you have some understanding of the subject area under study and why you have chosen it. In time you will make new friends and these friends will be your advocates and comrades. Many of them will become lifelong friends. Trust in yourself that over time you will build more self-confidence and network more easily.

Course delivery at university is complex, from the academic syllabus through to the methods of delivery on campus, off campus and virtually. There will be occasions to interact daily, whether that will be at lectures, tutorials, seminars, field trips or labs, practicals etc. for different disciplines. These activities will be explained in greater detail later in the next part of the book on page 36. By attendance and involvement in these academic exchanges, you will be presented with so many opportunities to extend your network. While many of your academic demands may require you to work alone, academic group work is an integral part of university life: hence the need to build your network. Building a network requires a proactive approach which extends far beyond the lecture theatre.

Making friends

You are bound to be looking forward to the next stage of becoming more independent, having more freedom, studying something new and exciting, meeting new people, doing what you enjoy.

Friends are important to all of us and we all want to feel that we belong. While at university, you will meet lots of new people on an exciting adventure, and make friendships that will shape your student life and provide fun and joy in the good times and offer you support in the difficult times.

Making new friends only happens with effort. Some barriers to making this effort can include spending a lot of time commuting to and from the campus, or family and employment commitments. Spoken English language skills often inhibit international students. Financial pressures may also be a consideration, as often students find themselves spending any spare time working part-time to fund their educational experience. However, if you search deeply, you will find lots of events on during the week and weekends which might fit with your busy schedule, and many of these events are free.

The familiarity of the school experience will no longer be available to you. Decision-making on all aspects of your university life is in your control and you will need to make many life-changing decisions in your first year at university. Unlike your younger days where events were organized and participation was encouraged by school/family/community/clubs, this time the responsibility lies with you to engage. Reach out and get involved.

The Students' Union

Attending social events organized by clubs and societies will ease the transition to making new friendships. Research shows that students who join clubs and societies in the first year of their university experience tend to settle in quicker to their new environment and have a better academic experience.

Getting involved in the social aspect of university life is vital both in terms of your personal and professional development. It is through such involvement that you will make relationships which ultimately will serve as blocks not only to build lasting friendships but a network of contacts that you will retain for life. These networks will help you to build your career, unite you across continents and cultures, and give you confidence to break into and adapt to new territories as you make your journey in a world challenged with rapid change.

Check out what is available to you at the Students' Union. There you will find all you need to know about clubs and societies that interest you. Societies are set up for the personal and professional development of the student body attending university. Such societies spread across the arts and the sciences, hobbies and interests, and universities cater for all interests. Discipline-specific societies are popular, and an easy way to connect with colleagues from your course. Likewise, sports clubs attract students with common playing interests both on the pitch and in supporting roles off the field. There is something for everyone.

If your interest is not catered for, you may consider approaching the office to set up a new club or society. That will read well on any CV when it comes to the job application process. Persist to find something of interest to you.

Living life at university offers so much more than an academic experience. An engaged social experience allows you to expand and grow in an environment which encourages freedom of expression and movement while developing lasting friendships and networks for life.

Try to make an effort to attend something each week to develop your network and meet new people. Nobody can, should or will force you to join anything.

Your involvement is entirely up to you.

Living at home

In recent years there has been a significant increase in students studying in England making long daily commutes to university from their family homes. A variety of factors, including financial and cultural barriers, influence decisions to move away or stay at home. For most, staying at home is, for the most part, to cut costs, but unfortunately this may also have negative effects on both academic and social life. Often lectures start early in morning, necessitating very early rises and expensive commutes. Likewise, living at home presents barriers to students who would like to engage in social activity and join societies and clubs at the university, which mainly meet in the evening and sometimes at weekends. Cultural issues may affect international students, who may be living with a relative they don't really know. Family can often be an added pressure on mature students.

But there are advantages too. If you are living at home, you may be fortunate enough to have most of your expenses covered. You will need to give some thought as to how you might contribute to the household in return. That might be in gardening, cooking, cleaning, shopping, looking after a sibling or maybe an elderly or dependent relative. Living at home and sharing as an adult in your traditional family home presents its own problems. It can become difficult to abide by rules at times, when there are conflicts of interest regarding standards of hygiene, cooking and so on. Spare a thought for everyone in your family unit and try to discuss how best to manage sharing as a mature adult.

If you are living at home and have a long commute to your university, you need to make this time work for you. Students are often not aware of the costs or time that travel will take. If travelling by train or bus, you could listen to a relevant podcast or lecture, organize your notes, revise material or work on assignments.

Living away from home

Many students live away from home and this move can be a source of considerable stress to begin with. It is a very expensive undertaking and many things need to be considered to find the ideal accommodation, particularly if England is not your home country and you are not familiar with the geography of the region in which you will be living and studying.

You may have never lived away from home before and are concerned about where you will live and who you will live with. Many anxieties exist: finding the right accommodation, the pressures of fitting in within your new environment and anxiety around making new friends. Whether you are living at home or away, there are many challenges facing you, but remember that you are one of many students experiencing the same feelings.

Settling into accommodation

Location is most important consideration when selecting accommodation, which may be on or off the university campus, depending on availability. Is the accommodation located close to the university or on the campus itself? If not, can you walk, cycle or take public transport? Is the area safe, well lit and secure? Is it situated in a basement or on the ground floor or first floor?

You will need to work within your budget and understand how the accommodation will be paid for together with allowances made for travel and subsistence.

Consider who you might live with. Who decides this? Sometimes this is outside your control and is dictated by the university. For some, this can be problematic as you may have never met your new housemate, and personalities, views, values and standards may also clash. On the other hand, you may not wish to share with friends or existing acquaintances or referrals through friends. You may want to branch out and embrace change from the start. While some problems are encountered in such a transition, most students can sort out their issues quickly and can also seek the advice of university staff/wardens who are assigned to oversee the smooth running of either on-campus or off-campus accommodation (the latter being more common today).

If you are sharing, it is wise to start as you intend to continue. In other words, set some ground rules such as the cleaning of the common living spaces and common appliances used, storage of foods and use of heating and electricity. The utilities are often included in the campus accommodation offered. Check this out with your university accommodation office.

It is only in private rented accommodation that you are likely to be responsible for bills. If students opt for private rental, they can seek help from the university accommodation office to find suitable agencies.

England can be a cold place in winter and so bills will accrue very quickly. If you are not in the know regarding these bills, it is useful to have a conversation with the energy suppliers about the size of your accommodation and typically what usage might be expected and how much the bills might be. They will have energy-saving tips which might lessen the financial burden. When you settle into university life you will also pick up tips from fellow students and find the best deals and discounts going through the Students' Union at the university.

It is important to consider how close you will be to the student social life both during the week and at weekends. This activity could be on campus, near the campus or perhaps in city centre areas. Newer university buildings are often located some distance away from the action spots and can in turn be quite a distance from your accommodation. This is also essential to consider if you are spending time studying in a university abroad over the course of your studies.

If you are living far from the campus or generally far from the social venues, you will need to have a reliable and safe public transport system to get you home late in the evenings. Your physical whereabouts is important to those who care about you. It's a good idea to have some kind of a check-in system with a few friends to ensure that everyone stays safe and that sensible precautions are taken to keep you safe. Straying from groups late at night is unwise. If you can, try to reach an agreement with your group that you will look out for each other when you can.

Rental agreements and leases will need careful scrutiny. International students will need a guarantor if they are not in university accommodation. This can take longer to sort out, so try to allow enough time. Read everything carefully before you sign. Penalties are imposed for breaking rules, which can cost you your deposit. Worse still, it may mean immediate eviction. When accommodation is provided by your university, sanctions will be imposed for inappropriate behaviour or abuse of university property, which will be brought to the attention of the authorities at the university. On occasions this can result in expulsion from your course. Check out the fine print on all agreements.

Respect your neighbours – you never know when you will need them or when they will need you. Be polite in your dealings. Spare a thought for families living in the university area who are trying to raise children and lead normal family lives. Student groups are often not welcomed with open arms when they move into a community. This might be a time to consider how you can integrate with the community and maybe reverse any preconceived ideas your neighbours might have about university students living in their area.

Homesickness

Many students are homesick. Homesickness can happen whether in the family home or living miles away from home. Within the home, the structures are different and the regular daily routine has been changed irrevocably. Uniforms are no longer worn and there is nobody looking over your shoulder regarding attendance and submission of material for assessment. You choose to attend or not to attend, and this varies due to the irregular nature of the academic day at university. Study patterns can be most erratic and you will require a strong sense of discipline and self-direction. Believe it or not, you will miss the regular questioning of your movements which happened during your last school experience, whether that was positive or negative.

Homesickness away from home is the one we can most identify with. Your living environment should be as friendly and stress-free as possible. Sharing accommodation with people you may have never met before, often with different standards and values, can in itself be daunting. It is vital to set some boundaries and rules to enable all sharing to make the environment a safe, clean and reasonably happy place to live. This is not an easy task but one that needs to be tackled early on to avoid unnecessary friction.

Ways to overcome homesickness include involvement in clubs and societies, charity work, part-time paid work or getting involved in the organization of events run by the Students' Union or the various academic departments.

By taking ownership and responsibility of your own journey and becoming involved in student life, most of your concerns will pass without too much complication and you will welcome the new start. What part you play will determine the end result.

Some essential life skills

Whether you live at home or away, if you don't know how to cook, now is the time to learn.

Cooking is a life skill and one you need to develop for many reasons – and the principal one is to help you to manage your finances. Research also consistently spells out the need to move away from processed foods, which over time can have detrimental effects on both our physical and mental well-being. Good natural ingredients are readily available and add to making your diet healthy and nutritious.

We all need to work to a budget. Making a large pot of a nutritious meal is highly recommended as this can last you a few days and works a treat when you come in from a long day's study – or indeed an evening of entertainment – particularly good in the long winter evenings in England. Students who are unprepared tend to waste their budgets on takeaway foods consumed late at night and all in the one night! If this happens to you on a Monday or Tuesday evening, you will have a hungry week ahead of you.

The big bugbear of all students is cleaning. Unfortunately, that job goes with the territory too. You will need to invest in a few simple cleaning products and set about doing a big clean-up once a week. If sharing, you can draw up a rota and look for buy-in from everybody. Once everyone knows their roles in the clean-up, they usually oblige. If not, deal with that problem quickly, as good hygiene is essential to healthy living and guarding against infectious diseases.

How a university works

Research, along with teaching and learning, is the core business of university education provision. It can be described as discovering new knowledge and insights, building on existing knowledge and discovery, establishing how experts view their subject discipline, how it is viewed by others and how it is documented in a credible and ethical manner for world reference and use. How this new discovery is interpreted by society in general, industry and the media, and how this research is funded, is important in the overall context of its application and value to society.

The value of research to our society and how it has revolutionized the way we live life is evident all around us. Some of the many benefits we enjoy today include discoveries such as: organ transplants, artificial intelligence, the Internet, genetic engineering and the discovery of penicillin and vaccines and the many other breakthrough drugs in the treatment and prevention of serious disease.

Research can lead to many unexpected discoveries and theories which shape and reshape the world around us. In the search for one answer, many other accidental rich discoveries are made. Research has its own language and each area of enquiry fits into its own academic style of writing which differs from discipline to discipline, attracting different terminology across the various subject areas.

The level and type of research you engage in will vary from university to university and from discipline to discipline and from person to person. However, this will become a central part of your university work in the final year in particular. Guidance on how to conduct research is available through the library services at all universities, and workshops are regularly offered to assist students in this regard. Your lecturers and mentors will also guide you in lectures and tutorials.

Over time, you too will become more proficient at conducting research, starting out by gathering information, and progressing to evaluating and engaging critically with its content in the context of academic argument, credibility of sources and your stage of learning.

You may have the opportunity to work with leading professors in the first year of your academic experience. Many students tend to focus on the number of lecture hours associated with a particular course and it takes time to understand that this is only one part of the academic schedule. Tutorials form a core element of the academic day, where students gather in small groups to interact with researchers and engage in academic debate surrounding the many complex theories which are covered in lectures but need considerable smaller group discussion to understand. These smaller groups are referred to as tutorials or seminars and are an ideal platform to interact with researchers and your peers and engage in academic enquiry, debate and opinion. These tutorials will influence your own interpretation of theory and its application relevant to the topics being researched at a given time.

All universities foster research and innovation and offer many supports to students who actively engage with their disciplines. They also support those who wish to reach further and develop new ideas into business ventures. Many students set up new businesses and this activity is warmly welcomed, with workshops held over the course of the academic year to assist.

Diversity

Unlike where you grew up, went to school or had your friendship group, you will now be engaging with people from across the country and the globe from more diverse backgrounds and cultures. Be prepared to immerse and challenge yourself with thinking about things through the lens of others.

Difference in culture brings a wealth of experience, inspires creativity, develops sensitivity and brings new insights to solving problems. Diversity enhances personal and professional growth and understanding. The integration of diversity can sometimes be problematic at the beginning as we grow to understand the extraordinary benefits which arise from working in groups which mirror the diversity that we experience in our workforce today. Graduates are sought for their ability to problem-solve across different cultures.

Culture and diversity will be discussed in greater detail in Part IV, 'Health, Identity and Society'.

Different systems

The university system is very different to the school system you have come from (see Table 1). It operates by a different set of rules and regulations and it is your responsibility to find out what this means for you and how you can adapt to the changes you will face through your university years.

Table 1 School and university are very different

At school	At university
Communication involves three parties – student, parent/guardian and teachers	Communication involves two parties – student and university
Familiarity with places and people	New faces and new places
Old friends network exists	New friends
Student lives at home or boards at school	Student may live away from home for the first time
Attendance is compulsory and monitored	Attendance is mostly voluntary
Study is imposed and monitored	Student chooses when and where to study
Financial responsibility generally rests with family	Financial management rests with the student
Teachers know student by name	Student is unknown to lecturers
Regular homework is assigned	No fixed pattern
Teacher asks for homework/assignments	Student is seldom asked for coursework/assignments
Teacher advises	Student seeks out advice
Small classes	Large lectures
Discipline is enforced	Adult behaviour is expected
Excuses are tolerated for unfinished work	Deadlines mean deadlines
Problems are identified early	Pace is faster and problems escalate quickly
Student is informed about rules and regulations	Responsibility lies with the student to find out the rules and regulations

Some of the significant changes between school and university can be evidenced in:

- changing relationships
- independent learning and critical thinking

Changing relationships

At school the relationship is between your parents/guardians, the school and you. At university, the relationship/contract is just between you and the university. Strict rules apply and you will have to deal directly with all issues that may arise. It is up to you to engage. You choose, and by choosing you have to deal with the consequence of your choices. Parents/guardians have no rights to information about your performance and will not be informed if you don't attend your lectures, don't turn up for examinations or don't hand in any coursework that is demanded from you. Likewise, nobody will make contact to praise your academic efforts and to proclaim your successes. Your academic results will be disclosed to you and to you only.

Universities will not engage with enquiries from parents/guardians as to your academic or social progress, except in very exceptional circumstances or where you have made a formal request for contact to be made with your parents/guardians regarding some aspect of your university experience.

In fact, the stark reality of it all is that if you choose to, you can do what you like, when you like and how you like – it is your journey and your call.

Your relationship with your family will also change over the course of your time at university. You are being forced to make all decisions yourself without influence or interference from others. Relationships change and family dynamics will alter as you grow and develop. If you are living at home, you may find that this can become problematic, as you may have to account for your movements unlike some of your peers who are living away from home. If this is you, spare a thought for those who pay the mortgage/rent and the bills. Living in harmony requires a lot of effort.

Student fees are not just for tuition, but for the whole university experience. Seek to access what is available to you. These interactions will contribute to progression to your next phase of personal and professional life.

We can now see, from the outset, why it is so important to take ownership and responsibility for this journey. Make it yours; be an active driver in your own destiny.

Independent learning and critical thinking

Independent learning at university is about taking control and ownership of your learning journey. You will be expected to manage this process at university. You will not be asked for homework. Attendance is mostly voluntary at university; study times are chosen by the student but deadlines are absolutely set in stone. Missing deadlines means loss of time, money and marks.

Different teaching and learning styles are adopted at university and the student is led more to an emphasis on understanding and critical and analytical thinking rather than learning and regurgitating facts and the opinions of others. You will be invited to critically appraise material and present your own views on your findings.

You will need to develop strong time-management skills as balancing university work can be problematic where there are conflicting workloads. You will work alone and in groups, and in time you will learn a new vocabulary relating specifically to the terminology of your discipline. All disciplines have a different lexicon and over the course of the first semester at university you will become more familiar with the new terminology. You will be guided on the style of academic writing and engage with the library services regarding the rules and regulations associated with writing in your chosen discipline. It is important to get to grips with this early on so that you can apply these rules seamlessly to all your academic endeavours.

Things will move quickly at university. You will be exposed to more material in a shorter space of time. In the beginning lectures may be very challenging, but this will settle. What is important is to attend everything that is relevant to your course, be that lectures, tutorials or any other interactions (these are explained in greater detail in the 'Academic activities' section in Part II). If you miss lectures, it is difficult to catch up. Students are often tempted not to attend because of feelings of incompetence, but all the advice is to keep going and make that extra effort as with time things will fall into place for you. Sometimes many students might find the same problems arising. This might be something which you could raise with your personal tutor and/or class representative. Class representatives are elected each year to represent specific student classes and to escalate their problems as one voice to the various offices, whether they are rooted in academic or social issues. This is a very effective way of getting problems sorted quickly.

University examiners seek to find strong and distinct engagement with academic material, evidence of critical and analytical thinking, an ability to interpret theory and to adhere to process, ultimately leading to the application of theory in a professional manner. At university we learn how to learn, and it is this ability to learn and to engage with information in a critical and analytical way that prepares us to adapt to an ever-changing and uncertain world ahead. Becoming an independent learner is about active learning and taking control of the learning process. It is an incremental skill with the seeds well planted in your first year at university.

The tutoring system

Most universities have a tutoring system. You will be advised how this works at your university during your orientation. This service is provided to guide and mentor you through your time at university. In most cases, tutors are drawn from the academic staff but on occasions may come from the administration or student advisory services.

As soon as you are aligned with a tutor, make an appointment to meet as soon as you can. Find out the preferred method of contact and how often you should meet. Tutors are there for your benefit and welfare, and issues raised are treated confidentially. This is an important relationship. Tutors act in your best interest both for your academic and social development.

Tutors are experienced practitioners and are also your first point of contact when you encounter stressful situations that are difficult to overcome. If you encounter a stressful situation that you are finding difficulty resolving, it is important to engage quickly. Dealing with problems early on means that you can get the appropriate support and service, ultimately leading to more positive outcomes. If you find that your worries are negatively affecting your personal, social or academic development, then it would be prudent to talk to your tutor to try to establish the most appropriate university service that can meet your needs.

Why students withdraw from courses

Unfortunately, thousands of students do not complete their studies at university, mainly because of mismatched expectations. This figure represents more than 120,000 students and is growing. Dropping out of courses brings economic and social hardship. Universities invest in providing support for student retention, which includes both academic and social support.

Students drop out of courses for many reasons:

- Wrong course choice
- Lack of commitment
- Academic difficulties
- Social difficulties
- Financial worries
- Concerns about careers
- Under-preparedness in subject areas
- Lack of motivation to make use of student services

In the case of mature students, many drop out of courses due to the heavy time demands placed on them alongside conflicting family and work commitments.

Wrong course choice

Picking the wrong course to study presents as one of the greatest problems with students who drop out during or after the first year of their studies at university.

The depth of study in your chosen area at university means that you need to be very comfortable with the overall subject area and have a genuine interest in building your knowledge and conducting research in this area. Success in your subject area will depend largely on how deeply you engage with the academic theories and applications, and to do this you need a genuine interest and love of the subject area which aligns with your academic progress and your mental well-being over the course of your time at university. That said, many students fail to recognize this in their early years and continue to struggle through to complete their studies in very unhappy circumstances. This is difficult not only for the student but for their family and friends, who worry about their mental health and their growth and development as contributing citizens under such pressured situations.

Lack of commitment

By taking ownership and responsibility for your own journey and becoming involved in student life, most of your concerns will pass without too much difficulty. However, you must play your part and make it happen.

If you want to succeed in your studies, you need to be present and active and engaging with all the academic demands of your course. That means that you commit to attend all lectures, tutorials and any other workshops, laboratories or such like that are set up to help you comprehend theories, concepts and applications relating to your studies. Most universities engage in considerable continuous assessment together with formal examinations. The need for consistent commitment is a key element in a consistent academic performance and grading.

Academic difficulties

Many students find the transition to university overwhelming in terms of the jump from the very directed learning process at school to the independent learning process at university. However, universities don't expect that you will make this leap overnight and to this end centres for academic practices are set up to help students cope with the different academic demands.

Grading criteria set at university will differ greatly from the school experience. It can be difficult for students who achieve high grades at school to accept that these grades do not automatically transfer to high grades at university. If this happens to you, search to find the reason for this in feedback from the assignments and help from fellow students, lecturers and your tutor.

Workshops are run for students in areas such as: essay writing, team working and learning, time management, reading and note-taking, mathematics and English language support, together with the use of library and referencing guidelines. These are outlined in greater detail in Part III.

Some students may feel that it is a sign of weakness to use these services but universities recognize the need to maintain high standards and this is why they facilitate such workshops. It makes perfect sense that anything that can help you achieve greater understanding and higher grades has to be beneficial for all concerned.

Believe in yourself. There will be twists and turns on this journey.

Social difficulties

Many studies have been carried out regarding the issues of settling into university, and social difficulties continue to present high on that list. This has been covered in greater detail in the section 'Fears and expectations' on page 2.

All of us, young and old, want to fit in, to belong, to be part of a community. Your university is a community – a community of scholars, a community of learning, a community of growth, a community of friendship, a community which when embraced with effort will guide and shape your path through your adult life.

Financial worries

Financial pressures are always lurking somewhere in the background. Have you thought through how your years of study will be funded? Someone has to pay the bill and under the English system that's more than likely to be you.

You have probably taken out a big loan to fund this experience, so you need to ensure that you get some return on your investment. The management of finances can be complicated. Living at home has its own costs. When living away from home in rented accommodation with attendant bills, unexpected expenses which arise from time to time can set all your budget plans awry and cause serious worry.

A big problem at the start of the year can be the delay in receiving funds, and this coupled with demands for payment of accommodation and other costs can be most stressful for students. Loan payments can be delayed and access to money from overseas is not always instant. Students need to engage with the finance office, student services and Students' Union to seek advice.

Many students receive the drawdown of bank loans and grants in large tranches, sometimes months in advance. The temptation to spend freely when these funds arrive poses an additional pressure. It is important to make a sound financial plan identifying your intended spending, weekly, monthly and annually. Students need to be aware at the outset that the ongoing expense of technology, books, travel costs and materials has to be provided for throughout the year.

Concerns about careers

What will I be? Who will I be? What will I be working at? Will I be an engineer, a doctor, a nurse, a physiotherapist, a computer scientist, a social worker or will I achieve anything if I study something that I enjoy but there is no obvious career path?

The truth of the matter here is that nobody knows where the jobs of the future will be, and this is changing and evolving at an unprecedented rate. What will be crucial are the skills and knowledge you develop on the journey that will make you flexible and adaptable to deal with the challenges that face the world and the workforce.

You will probably have a few careers and many jobs over the course of your lifetime. In this first year of study, while you might be a very focused student and know exactly where you are going or where you want to go, equally you may have absolutely no idea whatsoever where your path will take you. Commit to working consistently for your first year and time will present new thoughts and directions for you.

We will delve deeper into employment and the future of work in Part V of the book.

Under-preparedness in subject areas

This applies particularly to students who study the science, technology, engineering and mathematics (STEM) subjects, where there is a strong focus on the study of mathematics and usually a specific high-grade entry requirement. These courses demand an ability and willingness to solve problems using the underpinning mathematical concepts and skills. Genius is not a requirement, but a love and a sense of being very comfortable with these concepts is key to succeeding.

While the study of languages is predominantly concerned with the study of culture and literature of the mother tongue country, many students struggle with learning languages, particularly when taken up *ab initio*, i.e. without having studied it prior to studying the language at university.

There is university support available to you in all of these areas.

Lack of motivation to make use of student services

Support services on offer include: health services, language and mathematics support centres, disability services, dyslexia support, counselling advisory services, career counselling, tutoring, mental heath and wellbeing support, welfare, money and funding advice service, chaplaincy and other student advisory services. The Students' Union offers lots of support to students and will have an experienced team engaged to direct them to the appropriate service. While some Students' Unions at the smaller universities may not have these experienced teams in place, students should seek advice by making contact with their tutor who will be in a position to direct appropriately.

These are dealt with specifically in the 'University support services' section in Part II.

Some students find it hard to seek out support, particular those who are living with physical and mental illness, either themselves or in their families. Family separations and substance addiction can often present insurmountable barriers to reaching out for help.

In summary, there can be mismatched expectations. In this book we try to respond to these difficult situations by giving a detailed insight into what you can typically expect in your first year and far beyond.

Budgeting for your needs

Finance now plays a bigger role than ever in the journey through university as families struggle to work, to pay rents/mortgages, put food on the table and to maintain some semblance of normal family life. The recent pandemic has taken its toll on economies into the future, making it more uncertain and unstable for all. Students starting university will have been affected in some way by the global economic downturn and the rising cost of a university education, and the burden of student loans carried into careers by our graduates is onerous.

For the most part, in the school system, the family bears the financial responsibility of supporting the student, but at university things change. In some cases the family continues to offer some support. However, for the majority this is not the case and the student depends on loans, grants, part-time work and bursaries.

Regardless of where you live as a student, at home or away, being a full-time student is an expensive business. For those living at home, many make a significant contribution to their upkeep. You will need to address how bills will be paid throughout your university years, but more specifically in your first year.

Student loans are generally taken out by British students attending university in England. While this enables a university education, it comes with a big price tag which includes a long-term repayment plan. These loans have two aspects: tuition and maintenance loans.

Loans are paid in three annual instalments, starting on the first day. You must enrol with your university to trigger the loan. Payment can take at least three days to reach your account.

Interest is added from when you receive your first instalment. The interest rate is fixed at 1 per cent over base rate or RPI, whichever is lower, so currently this is around 1 per cent (which is cheap borrowing). Repayment does not commence until you start earning over a threshold, currently £26,575; if you never earn over the threshold, your loans are written off after 30 years.

It is important to work out how this loan can best serve your interests. You will need to establish the timing of the drawdown of the loans in the context of your overall budget plan, reflecting how you will accommodate your needs (not wants) over the academic year. The secret in making such a plan is to keep to it.

Public transport is expensive and adds up quickly so you must factor this cost into your overall budget, if it applies to you. Other obvious costs will need to be considered such as: technology, other equipment, stationery and books to support your study. A toolkit is suggested on page 19.

What type of heating and cooking facilities do you have? The question about heating applies in reverse if you are studying abroad in hotter climates as air conditioning costs can be equally expensive. Water and refuse rates, where applicable, should all be factored into your overall budget.

Look out for hidden costs such as childminding, additional transport costs to your home town, city or country, emergency trips home and medical expenses. Placement costs should also be taken into consideration. Take time to consider all these when planning ahead, while also trying to maintain a small contingency fund to deal with emergencies.

Cooking facilities are often limited to two rings and a microwave and may be shared by many. You will need to be creative in the kitchen and with your money. Good planning saves pounds. Guard against impulsive spending at the local convenience store on the way home from a gig as this could blow a whole week's budget in an evening. It is important to do your shopping early in the week and not when you are hungry. Make a list of what you need and stick to it. See 'Student Finance' in the Useful Links and Resources section at the back of this book for further information.

Starting Your University Journey **19**

As you begin to make friends and the academic year progresses, there will be a lot of discussion with fellow students about how vacation time in particular could be financially fruitful to offset the university bill in your second year. Many students become determined to spend this time abroad – however, availability of work is highly dependent on the state of the global economy as well as that in England, where international students have restricted employment rights.

Before considering looking for work abroad it is important to establish:

- if you will travel on your own or with others
- if others are fully committed to the plan
- if you will require a working or holiday visa
- if you require vaccinations in the travel zone
- your travel costs
- how you propose to fund flights, accommodation and additional living costs
- how you intend to cover your medical and travel insurance while abroad

If you are planning to work outside the country for the summer months, you will need to purchase your medical and travel insurance cover *before* leaving the country. If you don't have insurance before you travel, you will not get cover once you leave England/your home country. Accidents and emergencies can and will happen, so it is better to be well prepared. Special packages are available worldwide for students for this purpose.

Handbooks

Handbooks are vital pieces of your toolkit at university, and every course you attend will have one.

This is where you will find out information such as assignment deadlines, key dates and times, examination structures, rules and regulations and much more. You will need to read the handbook often as you will need to refer to it for direction as you begin to engage more with your course of study. Random references will be made to these handbooks but it is your responsibility to read them in full.

Handbooks will be dealt with in greater detail in Part II on pages 30–32.

Student toolkit

Every student should have a toolkit containing many essentials such as:

- course handbook
- budget plan

- debit card for contactless payments
- NUS (National Union of Students) card – offering discounts
- parking permit if commuting
- young person's railcard or similar
- study plan
- desk
- chair
- quiet place to study
- light
- equipment
- laptop (with Microsoft Office/other software which should be available at your university)
- mobile phone, Wi-Fi booster, USB/external drive
- access to printing (should be available at your university)
- secure bag to protect equipment
- services such as broadband
- bedclothes
- towels
- toiletries
- laboratory equipment/protective clothing (depending on your course of study)
- books
- stationery
- diary
- notebooks
- food staples
- household items
- cleaning products
- clothes for all weathers
- suitable footwear (waterproof and durable for long days)
- medicines
- personal items

Mature students

Returning to education can be daunting as a mature student who has been away from the study experience for many years. This can be further compounded by the fact that a higher proportion of students attending most universities come directly from the school system. Many challenges will present themselves, but try to value all that you will bring with you (for example, time management and independence) and look at how you can work with and learn from others regardless of age or life experience. It is the interests of any student group that will bridge any age barriers to achieve common goals. Challenges for the mature student group differ significantly from the more traditional student groups as the timing of the study can coincide with needing to care for young families and ageing relatives.

All universities operate electronic systems which facilitate registration, timetabling, examination and assessment fee payments. Various content management systems support online access to material and the use of virtual platforms are commonplace to deal with the changes in the delivery of learning in the twenty-first century. Your learning will more than likely consist of a mixed mode/blended approach which will offer both on- and off-campus experiences unless you are studying as a remote/distance learner without any visits to the physical campus. It is important to become proficient in the use of Microsoft Word, Excel and PowerPoint and to be comfortable using email and social media. Access to broadband is critical regardless of being a traditional university student or operating as a sole distance learner or in mixed mode. Mixed mode/blended learning is integral in the delivery of our education models today.

Some mature students deliberately enrol on remote and distance learning/ online programmes where all tuition and assessments are conducted at a distance, using virtual platforms and environments. When attending remotely as a learner, you will need to have a high level of self-discipline, be flexible and adaptable, and allocate a special undisturbed place and time for consistent study. Set goals to monitor and measure your progress.

Attending university is an expensive business and mature students can run into trouble if they don't plan well in advance. It is important to factor in direct costs such as fees, travel to placements and study materials over the lifetime of your course. You will also need to look at indirect costs such as childcare and transport, if they apply to you. Car sharing and help from friends and family can be invaluable.

Balancing time between work, study and family needs can also be difficult. If you have a young family, usual childhood illnesses crop up and in these situations a week is a short time. Consequently, deadlines can be missed. It is a good idea to try to get your work finished well in advance of your deadlines, especially if you have dependent relatives, young or old.

You will need all the support you can get, so get your family and friends on board. A consistent commitment to academic life may put a strain on relationships. Bring your family and friends on the journey with you. Discuss back-up plans. As you go, explain what you are doing and the impact this undertaking may have on all concerned and your present commitments. It's time to call in favours!

Working part-time

When making the decision to work part-time, due consideration must be given to assessing the academic workload associated with the particular course of study.

For some, part-time work may not fit in with a demanding university schedule and may negatively impact academic performance. On the other hand, it may be perfectly feasible to work for some hours each week without any conflict of interest. Most students look for work during summer breaks, some at home and many abroad. Such work develops a sense of responsibility and accountability, generates entrepreneurship and makes a good impression on any prospective employer.

Working part-time works well for many university students. When deciding about taking on this type of work, it is important to consider the impact it may have on your studies. It must be remembered that the principal reason for going to university is to study for a successful academic outcome. Some employers put pressure on students to work extra hours to retain jobs when it might not be feasible to do so.

When making decisions about taking part-time work, take into consideration the following:

- Flexibility to accommodate the academic demands of your course of study.
- How many contact hours do you have at your university?
- Do you have long days? For example, if you are studying science or engineering, you may run back to back with lectures, tutorials, demonstrations and laboratory work, which may leave you very little extra time to study.
- Think about the effects on your academic performance.
- What type of work is it – manual labour, service industry or online service?
- Where is it located? Do you have to travel, or can you operate from your home/study space to complete the work online?
- If you are travelling, are there hidden costs?
- What time of the day or night are you expected to work? Your sleep patterns may be negatively affected if you take on night shifts, which will impact on your ability to stay awake and attentive during the day.
- Safety may also be an issue if there are late night shifts involved.

According to UCAS (Universities and Colleges Admissions Service) most universities recommend working fewer than 15 hours per week. Many universities recommend that students engage in a maximum of 10 hours' part-time work. Norwegian research found that students who did some part-time work spent more time studying than those who had no part-time work. This may be too little for some and too much for others. A lot depends on how effective you are at time management (see 'Managing time effectively' in Part III).

There is a school of thought that your main efforts to make money should be centred around your vacation time rather than your term time at university. Conversely, most universities recognize the need to work. Some courses facilitate this by blocking the timetable on campus to two or three days a week. Work on campus is particularly beneficial. However, the practical and real issues of finance must also be considered. Given recent world events and recession, the availability of any type of work may be a serious cause for concern regarding the ongoing ability for students to finance their academic endeavours.

Concluding paragraphs

The university system is very different to the school environment that you have come from. Adult behaviour is expected and discipline is rarely an issue. Communication takes place between you and the university and this rule will not be broken unless in very exceptional circumstances. You are about to become the decision maker in all that you do. Nobody will follow you to find out where you are or what you are doing. Study patterns are chosen and set by you alone – but deadlines are set in stone with severe penalties applied for late submission of work. The study timetable is yours. You won't be chased for assignments or to study for examinations. It is up to you to become informed and find out the rules and regulations that apply to your university in general and your course/discipline/school/faculty within the university.

It is your responsibility to find out the academic demands placed on you and how to juggle the many deadlines across many subjects within different disciplines. The system in itself is complicated with larger classes and days which are generally loosely structured. You monitor your own progress, hence problems can escalate quickly. The structures vary from university to university, so it is important that you understand what structure applies at your university from the outset.

At university, lame excuses will not be tolerated. If technology fails on you, you will be expected to have a contingency plan to call on and have your work backed up and saved to a few places for easy retrieval. You will make your own mistakes, but you will also find the solutions. It is essential that you make early contact with your tutor, who can help you to make a smooth transition to your new world in the adventure of learning and find optimal solutions to the challenges you face, whether they are social or academic.

In Part II of this book, we will bring you to life as a '*Fresher*' and look at the various activities that you might encounter on a typical day. We will look at ways you can make your new environment your place of learning and discovery by gaining an understanding of the academic demands of your engagement. We will also explore the student services which are available to you, and more importantly how to use them to your best advantage.

Troubleshooting section

Top tips
- Get your finances sorted out
- Make contact with your tutor
- Read your handbook
- Attend everything you possibly can

This could be you

I am unhappy with my course choice

Dig deep to find out the reasons for this. Is it the subject area? Is it the pace at which it is being taught? Are you attending all your lectures and tutorials? Have you given it a fair chance? Are you seeking out help from the university services? Find out how your peers are adapting and try to form a study group to help you better understand the course content. Talk to your tutor.

I want to change my course

This is not as easy as it sounds. Some students think that once they are inside the university of their choice, moving will be easy. In spite of what you might hear, it is never easy to change courses. It is dependent on so many things, such as: entry grade requirements, level of laboratory work and availability of laboratory places, quota of students on the course, university rules, faculty/school rules, governing body on teaching and learning, local directors of teaching and learning, and general policy guidelines. Where the course is multidisciplinary and two or more schools in the university are involved, moving course is even more problematic. Talk to your tutor.

My loan money has not arrived

Many students find themselves in this situation. Go to the Students' Union/ Student Advisory Services office and ask for advice. They will be able to direct you to the appropriate office at the university. Talk to your tutor.

International students

English is not my first language

Your standard of English and command of speaking and writing the language is key to your overall success at university. You may have passed the minimum language requirement for entry but that is very different to being comfortable speaking and writing academically in the language. If you are falling behind in your studies because of your English, you must seek out help as soon as possible.

Take all the advice you can get from the academic services at your university in this regard. Look for language support laboratories which are readily available for your use. Making friends with native English speakers will develop your confidence and ability to communicate in the language. Get involved in university life. Talk to your tutor.

Things are very different in England

Pay particular attention to induction and orientation at your university. Things will be different from your home country regardless of your first language.

Familiarize yourself with all the rules and regulations and identify gaps which may cause problems for you. The earlier you identify these gaps, the quicker they can be remedied. Seek clarification in areas of ambiguity. Talk to your tutor.

Building employability skills

University is about much more than an academic qualification. When you graduate you will need a good degree and other experience, qualities and skills to differentiate you from other well-qualified graduates.

- Get involved
- Take ownership and responsibility for all that you do
- In making choices, you must be prepared for the consequences

Part II

Making it Your University

In this part of the book we will focus more on how the academic year is structured and what day-to-day life might look like, giving explanation to the various academic activities you will encounter during your time at university. This part will detail the function of handbooks and their relevance to your studies. It will also deal with the student services available to you, tying in with the tutoring system which has already been introduced in Part I on page 13.

We will divide this part into the following areas:

- Freshers and pressures
- Structure of the academic year
- Delivery and assessment
- Academic challenges
- Handbooks
- Absences from university
- Communicating with your university
- Tutor system
- Class representatives
- Academic activities
- Examinations
- Grading system
- Independent study time
- University support services
- Drawing on your personal resources

Freshers and pressures

Freshers are defined as students starting their first year at university, and typically each university sets aside a period of settling in, commonly referred to as 'Freshers' week'. This is an exciting time where you are coaxed, enticed, sweet-talked and inveigled into signing up for deals with banks, Internet providers, clubs and societies, all to trade for a burger and chips or a slice of pizza or a £10 cash incentive if you strike the jackpot! Needless to say students love the freebies and find themselves joining everything in that first week, but in time this frantic activity settles down and gradually you begin to pick and choose what suits you and your needs best.

You may also find yourself supporting particular causes in this week of enthusiasm. Guard against joining too quickly as you could find yourself amidst a large student protest. It is useful to remind yourself why you might support or oppose that cause. Are you following the crowd or are you truly committed to the cause?

During this week many extra events are put on to get you out and about and socializing with others. The fun is infectious across campus and the fever spreads to the more senior student community who, with staff at the university, oversee the organization and planning of these events in conjunction with the Students' Union office.

Freshers' week is fun, a time for laughter, a time where new chapters begin, a time to get involved. It brings a new-found freedom to your day and night, a freedom that you may never have had before. With that freedom comes the responsibility of making it work for you.

This is a time to be adventurous, to move outside your comfort zone, ask questions and attend some of the many events which are put on solely for your engagement and enjoyment. The Students' Union office will have a full list of these events. This office is also a great place to find out the best deals around on anything from stationery to travel, technology, gigs, clothing and much more. Those working in this office are usually senior students who know the ropes and are there to help you find something to suit your interests and needs. Try to engage with them in a meaningful way to maximize your opportunity and get to know what is happening on your campus.

You will need to be proactive and take the leap to explore new interests and meet up with other students from diverse backgrounds. Freshers' week is a time to enjoy and you will be surprised if you make an effort from the start. Research tells us that students who engage more in campus activities settle in better into university life and are more likely to have a better first-year experience. Check out noticeboards and social media channels or the latest news and events postings at your university.

Structure of the academic year

At most universities in England the academic year is technically broken down into two semesters lasting up to 15 weeks each and some may run an additional summer semester. Typically, undergraduate students will engage in the autumn and spring semesters which will cover both course and examination/assessment components.

In some universities 'terms' are used to break up the year into teaching units, one before December, one starting in January and one summer term. These terms can vary in length but usually comprise a set number of weeks each. The following is a typical example of how these three terms could be broken up over the academic year:

- Term 1: eight to ten weeks
- Term 2: eight to ten weeks
- Term 3: six to eight weeks

Examinations may be set during and at the end of the year, regardless of the terminology used to describe the academic year structure.

The structure of the academic year will vary from university to university and even from faculty to faculty, department to department and course to course within the same university. Nursing courses, for example, are much longer as they combine teaching and placements. Academic staff have certain 'academic freedom' within universities to set their own rules in line with their disciplines, as is their right under the Education Act.

You will be guided through this process in the handbook(s) relating to your particular course of study at your university.

Delivery and assessment

The academic demands imposed on you at university revolve around three fundamentals in any course of study:

- Learning objectives and outcomes
- Methods of teaching and delivery
- Assessment

The learning outcomes are determined by the academic staff in conjunction with course directors and course committees, all of which can be at department, school or faculty level depending on the university.

Methods of teaching and delivery will vary from university to university and course to course, and will generally be outlined in the handbooks for all courses. This will be discussed in more detail in the section 'Academic activities' on page 36.

Methods of assessment also vary from university to university and course to course. In all cases coursework will be integral to your assessment together with formal examinations either at the end of semesters/terms or at the end of the academic year, or both. You can be assessed using various methods of continuous assessment from coursework assignments to practical demonstrations, viva voce and presentations.

No two universities or courses will be identical in their learning outcomes, modes of delivery or the associated assessment processes. Many factors influence this, including the academic freedom afforded to the academic community as described earlier, the huge variation in university and class sizes and the multiple methods of delivery and assessment of the curricula. No one size fits all.

Over your time at university, you will engage in the many academic activities which are explained on page 36. While this list is not exhaustive it is illustrative of the general type of activities you will encounter. These may vary in terminology and in application from university to university and from course to course.

Many judge the university experience entirely on lecture hours – more often referred to as 'contact' hours – and can be unaware of the many other day-to-day activities that will take place and how these activities impact on your overall experience. The lecture hours are only one part of your university experience.

Academic challenges

During the orientation period at your university, you will quickly be introduced to the academic demands of your course and your timetable will be clearly defined.

The level of engagement will vary from discipline to discipline and will also depend on whether your course of learning is multidisciplinary. If your course is multidisciplinary, there will be a bit of a balancing act required as different rules apply across different disciplines.

Technically all undergraduate courses are worth 360 credits, so equate to 3600 hours of study. The key difference is how that time is spent, i.e. timetabled sessions or independent study, as a lot of students spend less time studying independently than is expected of them.

At university the pace is faster than you are used to at school. The level of enquiry is different, the study load is greater and more challenging as many other demands are placed on you which can interfere with giving such commitment. Students expect studying to be different, but they are surprised by the amount of freedom and responsibility. Studying independently is often expected to be like doing more homework.

Problems can first arise where you find yourself in a troubled state about getting to grips with a particular subject and the temptation to skip a lecture or two is great. But this only compounds the problem. Within a short number of weeks, the teaching term is well under way and then you may enter a state of panic in the lead up to assessments or examinations.

Problems of this nature escalate quickly, and unlike school may go unnoticed by the university. You will rarely, if ever, get a chance to catch up on lectures you have missed. The secret here is to identify any academic difficulties at the earliest possible stage and work towards finding a solution, a solution which might rest with fellow students or with academic staff or with the academic support offered in the university services (detailed in the last section of this part on page 47).

You will need to find out:

- what deadlines have to be met in the first semester/term
- if deadlines conflict and how you might handle your study schedule to accommodate this
- when your first assignments are due
- when the first formal examinations take place
- the implications of meeting these deadlines, completing your assignments and sitting your examinations in the context of your end of year results

Handbooks

Every course studied will have a handbook designed for your constant reference, which is presented either in electronic or manual format. In this handbook there will be great detail on the rules, regulations and general information surrounding the particular course of study. This handbook is the key guide to how business is conducted at your university and will state this clearly.

When it comes to rules and regulations and to the world of academia, the university system is unforgiving. This is such an important fact for you to know. You must familiarize yourself as soon as possible with the contents of all handbooks introduced on your course, and there may be a few.

If you are studying subjects across more than one department in the university, for example a business department and a language department, then two sets of rules apply: one for the business department and one for the language department. The presentation of the handbooks will vary from university to university. If your course of study stretches across three different departments in your university then a further set of rules may apply.

Separate from these course handbooks, there may be a governing 'university' rule book or handbook. This will be identified at your induction/orientation. You must study the university handbook in the context of its relevance to your course of study and being a member of the university community.

The 'university' rule book is particularly important when dealing with matters such as discipline, plagiarism/academic integrity, examination structures and rules, academic awards, deferrals, graduations, requests relating to withdrawal from courses and long absences.

Handbooks are updated annually for all courses. Pleading ignorance of the contents of handbooks falls on deaf ears. It is your responsibility to obtain copies of all relevant handbooks, which are usually available online through the course pages on the university website or learning platforms.

Familiarize yourself with the regulations relating to your course of study. You will need to read them regularly throughout the academic year as new experiences relating to the design, delivery and assessment of your course of study are encountered. Examples of these handbooks are widely available on various university websites.

Typically, course handbooks will cover the following and more:

- Academic support
- Assessment
- Checklists
- Communicating with academics
- Course content
- Course requirements
- Coursework/assignment rules
- Deadlines
- Dealing with absences
- Details of tutoring/mentoring/advisory system for students
- Examination rules and regulations
- Examination structures
- History of the particular department(s)
- How to communicate with university offices
- Independent learning expectations
- Key dates
- Learning outcomes
- Location of administrative offices
- Marking criteria
- Medical matters
- Methods of delivery
- Plagiarism/academic integrity
- Referencing styles
- Resitting arrangements
- Staff details and contact times
- Subject/module choices
- Timetables

It is most important to remember that while you might look for clarification in a handbook relating to one department on some aspect of a subject/module under study, if the situation is unclear you should establish whether the same rules apply under any general university regulations or student charter. Talk to your tutor if this is a concern for you.

If different rules do apply, you will need to seek advice from your tutor, an academic member of staff, course coordinator, course director or student advisor to establish the correct path to follow.

Should there be a conflict of opinion on any matters of this nature, you should, at the earliest possible time, seek clarification in writing of the final decision reached and keep a copy of this for your future reference.

The handbook contains a unique set of rules, laid out to be adhered to, with penalties imposed when broken, often detrimental to your academic progress. Many marks are lost due to simple instructions that are not adhered to such as layout, word count, presentation, formatting and deadlines. Deadlines are deadlines and are not to be missed. Severe penalties can apply for late submissions, regardless of the academic quality and excellence of the submission. Rules rule at university and none of the excuses are tolerated that might have seemed plausible in your final years at school.

It is also important to check your university email account and content management systems daily for any advice or changes which are advised either from administrative or academic offices. So many students fail to read these notices which can pose unnecessary problems down the line.

Absences from university

If you are absent from your studies and this absence is negatively affecting your ability to attend university and partake in academic activities, you will need to notify the university, in writing, of the situation.

If students have a long period of illness their first point of contact is their personal tutor or health and well-being/student advisory services, where they will be guided to the appropriate office or person. This will also be addressed in the handbook. Some universities require students to complete an absence form. A medical certificate and supporting documentation will be required if the absence is prolonged or impacts on assessment. You can then apply for extenuating circumstances. Your personal tutor, student services or a Students' Union representative can guide you through the process. You should keep copies of all communications.

This situation should be advised as soon as possible and close to the time of the absence. Absences for illness will be received sympathetically by the university and in situations where there is a delay in submission of coursework or you are unable to complete formal examinations, the academic council will make every effort to offer special examination sittings. This practice will vary from university to university. Your handbook should set out this process clearly. If this happens to you, make contact with your tutor, who will be in a strong position to advise you of what options are available to you, taking account of your personal circumstances.

Late submission of records of absences will not be sympathetically received by your university, however. While different examination times and methods may be put forward to assess your learning and understanding of subject material, no allowances will be made for poor academic performance due to absence. Grades will be awarded on a merit basis only.

Some universities now have an attendance policy, and they may use attendance monitoring, which means that the university may follow up if you don't attend for a particular period of time, but this is not universal. For particular programmes (with professional accreditation) there may be a minimum attendance requirement. This will be detailed in the course handbook.

The situation is, however, more complex for international students, as their attendance has to be monitored to ensure compliance with visa regulations. All international students must maintain an overall attendance record of at least 80 per cent in order to comply with the Home Office UK Visa and Immigration (UKVI) section requirements for Tier 4 study visa holders. International students whose attendance falls below 80 per cent must be reported to the Home Office UKVI and their visa may be terminated.

Consult your handbook for special rules on absence at your university.

Communicating with your university

Each university will have its own unique way of communicating with you. The most likely form of communication from the university is email. This is usually *only* through your university email address, so it is important to check this account daily. It is also essential to keep your personal details up to date, as your address may change each year, and mobile numbers can change etc.

Some universities use texts to contact students, e.g. about issues such as cancelled lectures and campus closures. Important information is usually posted in your section of the online learning environment.

There are both formal and informal social media groups for courses and year groups that share information much quicker than through other university channels (e.g. about cancellations or changes to the schedule).

It is up to you to find out how communication takes place and how the system works for you. This can vary from discipline to discipline and due to different styles of academic direction and individual differences. Welcome again to academic freedom! You need to establish what form of contact works with your lecturers, course directors, tutors and any others who you may engage with over your time in university. This includes administration, technical support and the university support services. Your handbook may set out specific methods of communication for different activities.

There are many ways that you will make contact, such as:

- with your tutor
- at tutorials/seminars
- during and after lectures
- electronic and traditional noticeboards
- email
- face to face
- online learning and meeting platforms
- social media
- through the tutoring system
- content management systems

- virtual discussion boards
- virtual learning environments

While the deliverables may change, the time of submission may also change, and you are dependent on the cooperation of administrative staff to process your assignments. It is important to communicate to all staff you meet at your university with the same respect, be they security, administrative, academic or ancillary. Your university is a community: a community made up of many parts, a community united in its mission, and yet even in the largest universities it is small in its network. As you gain a greater understanding of many of the interactions that can take place at your university, it will become evident where and how cracks in the various communication channels could appear.

Communication with your university will be very different to the communication you have been used to at school. At university it is between you, the student, and the university. No third party is involved.

Prepare well before you engage. Ask yourself what the purpose of the communication is, and be clear about what you want to achieve from it.

What you do or do not do at university is your choice, however, you and you alone have to deal with the consequences of that choice. A more reflective approach to decision-making in the early stages of your life at university will reap rewards over the course of your study.

Tutor system

As discussed in Part I, most universities offer a personal and confidential tutoring or academic advisory system, but these operate in different ways. Usually you will be assigned a personal tutor or academic advisor for the duration of your undergraduate degree. The aim is that the tutor/advisor gets to know you, and vice versa, and that they guide you through your studies, often being your first point of contact if you experience any academic or personal challenges. They are also able to provide you with an informed reference once you graduate and start applying for graduate positions.

Systems vary between universities. You may have individual or group meetings in the form of taught sessions, or the meetings may be more like conversations. The aim is to support you to thrive; group sessions have the added advantage of helping you to get to know other students on your course. You can always book a one-to-one session (in person or online) if you have anything confidential to discuss. The contents of these sessions are strictly confidential unless the tutor advises a need to share information. They may do this if you agree to another university service such as health and wellbeing, counselling or academic services being involved. Tutors are people to discuss your hopes and aspirations with, to plan how to succeed in your degree, and to develop your additional skills and experiences to help you secure a graduate position. They may also have contacts in industry or academia that can be helpful to you.

Universities offer a wide range of student services to support and develop you academically, personally and professionally. It is a good idea to take advantage of these services. Your tutor or advisor can signpost or refer you to these services or you can contact them directly. Many students believe these services are only available to you when you have problems. This is not the case – many of the services are set up for your benefit to use throughout the university experience to help you maximize your opportunities towards success.

Class representatives

Every core student course group in university will have a class representative, known as a 'class rep' – a service for students run by students and supported by the university. The election of these class reps is often directed via the Students' Union.

Class reps are elected by their class peers in the course of the first few weeks in the first semester. Class reps are not elected because of their popularity, but more because of their desire and ability to understand how university works, to see things objectively, to actively listen, to work well with others, to voice the opinion of their class and to act in a responsible manner in representing these opinions to university staff and officers. While the position carries academic responsibilities, class reps are highly involved in organizing many social activities for the class.

Class reps have a very important role in communicating with staff at the university. Handling difficult situations at university can, at times, prove to be awkward business. If you find that you are having an academic problem, you can start by approaching the individual lecturer or course director, or you can use the available university tutoring/student advisory/counselling services. However, you may feel uncomfortable about doing this on your own for a variety of reasons.

Class reps or officers in the Students' Union can be most useful when it comes to students handling difficult situations or making complaints about matters that might arise over the course of their study. Complaints at university are often best voiced as one. Where there are valid grounds for a particular complaint regarding academic or administrative matters, it can be best to seek a group or class opinion on the arising issues. If a general consensus of opinion emerges relating to such complaints, the class rep can then become the voice for those complaints, working on behalf of the group/class with course coordinators/course directors/lecturers/university offices/committees and others concerned. While resolutions are not always immediately forthcoming, such efforts are taken seriously by university and course committees. The student voice matters at university.

Academic activities

The following list might help you understand how your day-to-day life at university is filled with many academic activities:

- Registration/enrolment
- Induction/orientation
- Modules
- Lectures
- Library
- Electronic systems
- Tutorials/seminars
- Guest speakers
- Laboratories/demonstrations
- Presentations
- Research
- Coursework/assignments
- Reading weeks
- Group work
- Academic writing
- Academic integrity

Registration/enrolment

When you attend university, you are required to formally register as a student. Payment of fees forms an integral part of this registration, which is generally automatically generated to the university's bank account for domestic students only. All students attending must register every year as a matter of course. Increasingly enrolment is online, rather than having to queue up at an appointed time, but it must still be done within a specific time period. You may have to register separately with the Students' Union to receive your Students' Union card. Your university student number is important and will be required when you submit assessments and so on.

It is essential that you register at the appointed time as fines will be imposed for late registrations and access to services such as the university support services, electronic systems, the library and online tuition will not be made available to you until the process is complete. Generally, student cards are issued following registration.

Please note that you will not be able to sit official university examinations if you are not formally registered. Likewise, final year students will not be permitted to graduate if they are not properly registered in their graduation year.

Induction/orientation

Each university will have its own unique way of introducing you to the university campus and its facilities, setting aside a number of days or weeks for this process. This period of orientation provides you with an opportunity to familiarize yourself with the campus, and can include:

- the location of the buildings you will frequent
- the library
- the type of systems the university employs
- how to communicate effectively with your university
- different communication methods
- the range of facilities available for your use
- modes of delivery of the syllabus
- student support services
- university rules and traditions
- key academic dates and events

Smaller local induction sessions may be held during or outside the formal larger university orientation period. These sessions are more course-specific and attendance is essential if you are serious about your commitment to study.

It is vital that you attend any orientation/induction sessions as it is here that myths are dispelled and fears are allayed, the beginnings of long friendships are formed, and confidence grows. Too often, some students make the mistake of thinking of these sessions as unimportant. Increasingly these early sessions are also used to help students create peer networks of support and they are key to surviving your first semester/year.

Modules

Modules are formally structured units of learning with specific learning outcomes which carry an academic value measured in credits, e.g. 10, 15, 20 credits. An undergraduate programme of study comprises a series of modules leading to 360 credits; full-time students will study for 120 credits per year and pro rata for part-time students.

Assessment varies from module to module; however, it usually takes place at the end of the module rather than at the end of the academic year. On successful completion of your first year, it is important to note that many modules in your second year together with your third/final year contribute to your final degree award.

On many courses you will take compulsory core modules and other option modules. At some universities, you may also be able to choose modules outside of your core course curriculum. Elective modules allow you to deepen your knowledge of the compulsory or option modules or can form part of a broader curriculum to explore subjects unrelated to your main subject area.

Lectures

This is the traditional tuition normally delivered by academics. At lectures you are given a broad account of the course or subject under study in your discipline. This process can take many forms, from the more traditional instruction in large and small lecture theatres and laboratories to the virtual experience across a variety of learning platforms.

The focus of the lecture is to introduce you to the fundamentals and the core teaching relating to a subject. You are then expected to research the topic under study and build on the fundamentals in your own time. This is the first point where you may feel uncomfortable about how to approach the task and the seeds of self-direction in the learning process are set.

Attendance at lectures is a basic university requirement and you should make every effort to be on time. It is good practice and good manners. While this attendance is generally voluntary and entirely within your control, some universities may impose the rule of compulsory attendance. Check this out in your handbook.

Occasionally 'in class' exercises may be conducted and collected which can serve as an attendance list by another means. Failure to attend such lectures may risk poor performance or even failure.

Academic concepts and theories are introduced and explored at lectures, but once dealt with are seldom repeated – hence the need to attend all lectures and develop good note-taking skills and listening skills. Administrative matters raised by lecturers will generally be raised once and once only. A typical example of this might be a deadline announced for the submission of assignment work.

You will need to get to know the individual style of each lecturer and this will become apparent quite early on. It is important to understand that each lecturer is concerned with his or her subject only and it is in this context that you slowly realize that your timetable needs to be managed carefully, juggling the demands placed by the various lecturers in the many subjects studied on your course.

Remember that the lecturer is also the examiner. Given this situation, obvious tips may be often given such as 'note this carefully' or 'this is probably the most important part of …' or 'students always forget that …' or 'what I find on examination papers is that students fail to recognize …'.

At first, you will find it hard to understand what information is significant and what is not. This is perfectly normal, and this skill will develop as you progress through the first year exploring further subjects and engaging in academic debate on the many opinions on these subjects. The lecture is only one of the many activities at the heart of your working week.

Library

The library is the cornerstone of all learning and an essential and an integral resource for all students attending university. The library can take two forms: that of the physical building or its electronic form, or a combination of both. It can be accessed both on campus and remotely.

You will be introduced to the library and how it works during orientation. Special workshops will be provided for new students. Particular emphasis will be placed on learning the university 'search' system. Physical engagement with the library exudes a scholarly air and envelops the magnitude of the world of discovery and learning. Increasingly, libraries include group study zones that have quite a different feel, while there will also be quiet study areas and areas where you can access a PC to work on. You can often book private spaces or group spaces to meet your needs.

You may feel intimidated on the first visits, regardless of location – on campus or online. You will find it difficult to know where to look for material, unable at first to discern the relevant from the irrelevant or the good from the mediocre.

Lecturers and demonstrators will guide you through this process by gradually introducing you to the key authors in the discipline of study. As you gain confidence in the subject area and become familiar with the key concepts and theories addressed by these authors, you will then begin to explore ideas further by reading and researching around the subject. This will happen over time as you incrementally acquire the skill of making good judgements regarding academic credibility.

The art of referencing academic work goes hand in hand with the library and with all writing in the course of your study at university. It is important that you understand the implications of correctly referencing academic work early on in your university experience. This can prove daunting for some. However, this should not be the case as the library and university support staff provide regular assistance to all in learning this art. Invest time in getting to know the system – it will pay dividends.

All courses will have reading lists, comprising some core essential reference books and some recommended reading. The library holds a limited stock of all books whether essential or recommended reading. Students who are there early get the best pickings, either within the library building or in many cases taking out books on loan for a number of weeks. Some students buy a limited set of core textbooks which may be required over a number of years of the course of study. Others join together and share the cost; however, the distribution and collection of these books in a shared system can be problematic.

Libraries impose fines on students for books which are overdue. Students must pay outstanding fines before being allowed to graduate with their year.

Electronic learning systems and support

Every university will have its own electronic systems which, in the first instance, cater for the administrative functions within the university.

These will typically include:

- registration
- timetabling
- examination systems
- grading systems
- fee payments
- academic awards

Various content management systems and electronic platforms are employed by universities to facilitate online access by you to academic material. Online teaching and tutorials can facilitate students whether on campus, at home or in a workplace. Much of the preparatory and follow-up work is detailed on these platforms, which can also provide opportunities for discussion about particular topics – and this can be a good way to engage with teaching staff and peers.

A blended learning approach to teaching and learning is the ideal option where both the traditional and electronic are used to support the learning experience. More sophisticated developments are evolving as we see further changes in the delivery of learning in our digital age.

It is possible that you can engage in university activity over the course of a given academic year, sit examinations and obtain results without your family being aware if you have attended university or submitted material for assessment. Almost all results are posted electronically and can only be accessed using a personal access code known only to you.

In essence, you can do your own thing for a full year at university and nobody may even notice. This is where the choice is yours, but the consequences are yours too.

Tutorials/seminars

Tutorials/seminars take place in small groups and are generally centred around your lectures. These are not to be confused with the tutor system referred to earlier. Tutorials/seminars can be facilitated by lecturers, teaching assistants or demonstrators who are appointed by the various course directors and committees. Tutorials offer you an opportunity to discuss issues which arise during the formal lectures but which due to time constraints can't be elaborated on at that time. They afford you opportunities for debate through interaction with academic staff where all work together to find solutions and avenues for further exploration.

Tutorials are an integral part of the learning process and students find them extremely useful in progressing to a deeper level of understanding in their chosen subject areas. Attendance is very often compulsory and students can be regularly assessed both on their attendance and on their level of interaction. Your handbook will guide you.

Students wishing to optimize the experience come prepared and so they are better placed to contribute positively to discussion. Tutorials can take different formats – for example, the science discipline may have practical elements quite different from the tutorials in the arts and humanities disciplines.

Guest speakers

Guest speakers are often invited to address the student body. These can be university, industry, subject-based, society or student-led, and like tutorials can provide opportunities to deepen the learning experience in a particular subject area. Some may be strictly informative while others take a more problem-solving approach, relying on student participation. All will provide networking opportunities focusing on building up relationships into the future.

Laboratories, demonstrations and practicals

Often referred to as labs or demos, these can vary in format and delivery and can be held in scientific laboratories, computer-based laboratories, small meeting rooms, on-site or field visits, and at various off-site locations. Generally facilitated by postgraduate demonstrators, these sessions offer students the opportunity to learn by practice, experimentation and problem-solving.

You will need to familiarize yourself with the various formats by carefully reading the associated course/university handbook(s). As with the lectures and tutorials, attendance may be compulsory and you should check your handbook to establish if this is the case.

Presentations

Presentations are becoming a more integral part of the academic experience at university. Students are regularly required to make presentations, individually or as part of a group. These presentations are almost always assessed as part of the annual examination process and can take many formats.

Good presentation skills are essential and transferable skills which are widely sought after in today's workplace.

Presentation and communication skills are addressed in great detail in Part III 'University Skills'. Workshops at the university in this area will also be made available to you as additional support.

Research

Research, like teaching and learning, is the core business of the university. It can be simply defined as finding out significant facts and information about a subject. It can be described as discovering new insights, new knowledge or combining existing knowledge, finding out what the key authors of a subject are writing about and how the subject is viewed and interpreted by academia, industry and society. The degree to which research is conducted varies and is usually determined by the academic demands placed on the student at a particular stage in the academic cycle of study.

Research can lead to new and unexpected discovery of theories and applications which contribute to the development and shape of the world we live in from social, cultural and economic perspectives. In the course of researching, the student reads to gather information, to analyse and interpret findings and to adopt an academic style of writing.

Reading is an integral part of research; it is a skill in itself and incorporates scanning, skimming, normal reading and close reading. Understanding is more important than speed. Students tend to learn this process in incremental stages at university.

In your first year, you may be taught by leading professors and researchers in the field of your chosen study. They may also facilitate seminars. When you attend tutorials, you will also have opportunities to interact with postgraduate students who work at the cutting edge of research in research groups.

All universities foster research and innovation from within and offer support to students who bring new ideas to successful business ventures through their research in the course of their university studies. It is not unusual for students to set up new businesses while in their first few years at university. Such activity is widely encouraged within the university and student community and workshops are often held to develop ideas.

See Part III 'University Skills' for more about research skills on page 66.

Coursework, assignments and portfolios

These are examinations by another name and can present in many forms including as essays, project work, multiple choice questions, presentations and portfolios, and may be examined as practical or clinical work, by oral demonstrations or as a body of written work. These are opportunities to apply theory, simulate professional practice and to consolidate learning.

The terms 'coursework' and 'continuous assessment' may be used interchangeably. This work is allocated a percentage of marks which contributes to the overall result within any course of study in the academic year. This is clearly set out in the handbooks for the particular course under study. Penalties are usually imposed for late submissions, and in some cases these can be quite severe, resulting in failure due to lateness rather than academic ability. If late submission of work is the sole reason for failure, the university will generally treat this as a breach of the university rules.

In certain circumstances, the student may be afforded an opportunity to resubmit. It can also be the case that a student may have passed the formal examinations at the end of the semesters/academic year but may end up having to change their summer plans simply because of a missed 'coursework' deadline.

It is important to recognize the value of keeping copies of all written coursework, whether in paper or electronic form. Backing up files on computers/laptops at regular intervals and on completion/submission of academic work will save disappointment and a lot of reworking at some stage of your university journey.

Adopting good habits early on pays dividends. You should also note that marks are, in almost all cases, awarded for the formatting and presentation of coursework. Don't waste them.

Refer to your course handbook(s) for rules relating to all of the above.

Reading weeks

At most universities, students are afforded reading weeks during each semester or close to examination time.

These weeks can give students time to hone their study plans for the remainder of the semester or year and to identify any university services which may help along the way. Usually, no formal lectures take place at this time. However, some universities may run presentations, orals and practical assessments during these weeks.

This time is assigned specifically for the purposes of reading up on course material, working on unfinished assignments and generally catching up on university work and taking time to reflect on your overall performance to date.

Group work

Students at university will have to collaborate with others, forming groups in which they work together to a common goal, often towards producing a report or assignment or building a product or developing a research idea.

It will be impossible for you to attend university as an undergraduate for three or four years and work alone. Interaction with others is a necessary part of the academic and social development of every student. Whether working in industry, the professions or business, working as part of a team is vital and employers rate it as a crucial skill.

Working in groups can often be quite difficult as it presents many challenges. On some courses students can self-select their groups, while on other courses this selection is imposed by course directors or coordinators. Both ways can prove problematic as groups must develop into teams before they can begin to work effectively together.

The discussion regarding the fundamental differences of working in groups and teams is a subject in its own right and is addressed in greater detail in Part III on page 60.

Academic writing

You may have memories of studying Shakespeare from school, and whether it was the sonnets or King Lear, Macbeth or Romeo and Juliet, many can probably recite passages at will. We could say that Shakespeare went about making his point in a rather complex manner, using heightened language which required significant work in its interpretation. So, to some extent, you entered into the spirit of the time, parsing and analysing passages for deeper meaning and finding ways of applying this to ordinary daily living either in its time or analysing its relevance to our own time.

If we transfer this concept to any study at university, for example science, language, business, law, education or health, we discover that each subject has its own particular language, its own set of words associated with that subject and/or profession. Like studying Shakespeare, you will become familiar with the language of your subject and take the time to learn to appreciate and understand the terminology and how it is expressed in your course of study.

Some students adapt quickly to the unique style of academic writing, but many find it challenging. Academic writing will be much more problematic for international students if English is not their first language. It is so important to seek out the services to assist. Get in touch with the Student Advisory Services, writing support services and your tutor.

Through the university library system, you can learn the art of academic writing by constant reading and reflection using:

- textbooks
- academic papers
- technical papers
- conference proceedings
- the academic work of other students
- attendance at different workshops

Academic writing is covered in greater detail in Part III 'University Skills' on page 67.

Academic integrity

One of the greatest and most frowned upon academic breaches is that of plagiarism, where students take the work of others and claim it as their own. You will be introduced to the art of referencing and the issue of plagiarism through the library services at your university. Workshops are run regularly for this purpose and it is most important to understand this system fully in your first weeks at the university.

Plagiarism is serious. It can mean failure or expulsion. In academic writing or presentation, all authors' work must be acknowledged.

Cutting and pasting from the Internet is not tolerated. Lecturers and examiners can tell very quickly when a student is committing this offence as they are expert in the field of their own studies. Software systems such as Turnitin are used by lecturers to examine students' work for plagiarism when it is submitted for assessment.

Other major breaches include:

- carrying and using mobile technology during examinations
- inappropriate use of social media and technology while conducting academic and university business

If and when sanctions are imposed for such breaches, the penalties that apply are severe. These are stated clearly in the handbook(s).

Examinations

Examinations take many formats throughout the year and at the end of the year. Students are examined over the course of the academic year through continuous assessment, which may be known as coursework and presents in many forms such as:

- analysing case studies
- analysing problem scenarios
- attendance and performance at practical demonstrations
- demonstrations
- essays
- multiple choice questions
- orals
- participation at tutorials
- portfolios
- presentations
- project work
- reports
- viva voce

A certain percentage of the overall academic grading for the year is allocated to this type of work and as deadlines are met and passed this work is corrected and the results are recorded. The marks achieved through this form of assessment are then filed into the individual student record, and at the end of the academic year are added to all other examination results, with a final grading being awarded to the student at this time.

If the student fails any aspect of this coursework, a second opportunity may be offered to resubmit. However, this is highly dependent on the nature of the subject under study, the reasons for the failure and the local rules outlined in the handbook(s) and any university rules pertaining to the particular type of continuous assessment in question.

In all examinations, whether coursework or formal written examinations, you will be required to submit a student identity card/number showing that you are a registered student at the university. Failure to produce this may result in lost assignments and refusal of permission to sit examinations. You should also note that unless you are formally registered as a student of the university you will not be permitted to partake in the formal examination process.

Table 2 The typical grading system

Classification	Grade	Percentage
First class	I/A	70–100 %
Second class (upper)	II.I/B	60–69%
Second class (lower)	II.II/C	50–59 %
Pass (some universities award a third-class grade)	P/III	45–49%
Pass	P	40–44%
Fail	F	39% and below

Grading system

The grading system may vary slightly from university to university, but Table 2 may be taken as a typical example of how the grading system can be broadly categorized.

To achieve 70 per cent or higher at university, you need to be at the top of your game. Only a very small number of students achieve these high grades. Sometimes students who have always had high predictive grades at school find the level of marking somewhat penal at university. Learning and the expectations are different, and skills developed at school are not directly transferable (e.g. regurgitating lots of information). Students can find moving from achieving consistent top grades to a lower second-class honours inexplicable. Should this happen to you, feedback from your assignment together with engagement with your tutor will help you identify problem areas.

On careful examination of the criteria set for grading of the examination, the student learns to understand that critical thinking with well-supported argument is rewarded at this level, rather than the regurgitation of key facts from a very broad but not necessarily deep base.

Pass grades vary from course to course and university to university. On many courses the pass rate is set at 40 per cent, but on some it is 50 per cent or higher.

It is vital that you check what pass grade applies to both your continuous assessment and formal examinations, and how grades are classified on your course. This information should be available in your handbook.

Independent study time

As you can see, your day is now filling up with lectures, tutorials, group work, demonstrations and other activities, but study time still needs to be found.

Managing your timetable and fitting in study time can be stressful and challenging. If you have a low number of contact/lecture hours, for example as an arts or law student, you will have to be more self-directed in your remaining hours, unlike your fellow engineering or science students who will have high contact/lecture hours with a more fixed schedule.

All students, regardless of their course of study, need to develop a consistent approach to study given the nature of the demand of assignments and other work set as part of the continuous assessment process. There is a nominal expectation of 1200 hours per year.

Some students enter university with little understanding of the level of study required in order to achieve academically. You will need a strong study ethos. You need to commit to a demanding academic workload and take full responsibility for your learning journey.

It is impossible to accurately gauge what study time is required as this will vary from student to student, from course to course, and by type of subject undertaken within any course of study. This will also depend greatly on how you learn and how you study, and the academic demands placed on you.

Trying past examination papers regularly can be a good check of how your study is going at any given time during the academic year.

University support services

Every university provides a unique set of services and support for all students attending. These services may be called different names and dealt with by different offices at each university.

These services are provided at many levels, all with the common goals of maximizing your social, professional, personal and academic development. It is important that you become familiar with all the services on offer in the university of your choice as the time will come when you may need some help or advice.

Seeking help is seen as a wise and forward-thinking move. Everyone needs help at some point in some aspect of daily life. The first step is to identify what help is required. The range of support services available include:

- accommodation
- financial
- academic
- career services
- chaplaincy
- counselling
- disability
- health services
- care leavers

- support centres
- personal tutoring/mentoring/student advice

Accommodation

Universities provide assistance to students who are in search of accommodation both on and off campus. Campus accommodation, where available, is limited and should be applied for months in advance of entry. Please check the accommodation section on your chosen university website for these dates.

Priority is given to first years. There are lots of private halls that students live in which are very similar to campus halls. There are also agencies that are approved by the university, sometimes based on campus. The university accommodation office keeps lists of various accommodation options, which are regularly updated.

Academic services

A range of free academic and associated services is available to assist you throughout the university experience, such as:

- writing skills
- study skills
- maths support
- English language support
- information technology training
- library skills
- research skills
- referencing skills
- critical thinking skills
- life and time management
- presentation skills
- stress management
- studying in groups
- teambuilding skills
- examination preparation

The development of these skills will greatly enhance your ability to perform and gain confidence in approaching the challenging learning situations ahead. These skills are also invaluable during work placements in industry while at university and later on when entering the workplace as a graduate. It is most important for you to identify areas where you might like or need to seek help and how to make the most of the available services. These areas will change over the course of your study path.

Career services

The careers service office in your university offers students advice on career planning, job searching, CV preparation, interview preparation and preparation for occupational assessments. Related services include the placements office, volunteering etc. – all ways to gain graduate skills. Advice may be offered at group workshops or by individual arrangement.

This office works with prospective employers locally, nationally and internationally and acts as a central point for recruitment of graduates in the university. Employers are happy to interact with students at regular intervals through recruitment fairs, prize-givings, guest lecturing, workshops and the showcasing of student work.

The office also liaises with graduates who often return to share their experiences and offer advice on career paths to students. If workshops are made available to you, it is wise to attend as many as possible. Given our competitive work environment, you must seek to perfect your CV, excel at interview and understand how best to fit with employers' needs both as a student and a graduate. This is covered in greater detail in the final part of this book, 'Looking Ahead'.

Chaplaincy

Universities offer chaplaincy services which seek to support all faiths and non-religious world views in the university community. Chaplains offer spiritual guidance to those who look for it and very often run seminars on related topics which you will be invited to attend.

Other social gatherings are also organized such as coffee mornings, lunches, parties, prayer sessions and interfaith gatherings. Chaplains offer a range of services and can be useful to international students, providing a safe space.

The chaplains may also offer confidential advice and guidance on many social, personal and academic matters.

Counselling services

A free and confidential counselling service is available to you at university if you run into academic or personal difficulties and need a helping hand. These issues may present as a defined personal problem or may be the result of other influencing factors in your environment such as family sickness, bereavement or a very untimely departure of a good friend, classmate or family member.

Scheduled talks on managing many of these issues also take place over the course of the academic year. These might typically include:

- mental health
- suicide
- drugs and addiction
- money problems

- eating disorders
- depression
- relationship problems
- personal safety
- dealing with anxiety
- loss or grief

You need to look for notices about general talks available which might help in a time of crisis. It is important to seek help early on with any problem you may be having as this will limit any negative impact on your ability to partake in academic and social activities while at university.

There can sometimes be a delay in getting appointments with the health and well-being/counselling and student advisory services. It is a good idea to see your personal tutor in the first instance. Universities are very aware of mental health issues, so 24/7 support is often available online through the university website. Your tutor or Students' Union service can also direct you appropriately.

Disability services

Students with disabilities are well catered for at university and there is usually a dedicated office which is responsible for this support. In the course of your application, you may have already disclosed any known disabilities, but records are not routinely transferred. You must make yourself known to the office concerned at the time of your registration so that all the necessary support can be put in place for you.

You will be assessed, and an individual support plan drawn up. You may be entitled to financial support, in the form of a disabled student's allowance.

Health services

Universities offer a confidential and free medical service to all their registered students, both domestic and international.

The health services promote healthy lifestyle habits and work closely with the counselling services offering advice on the physical, psychological and social aspects of student health. Information is also widely available in many areas including sexual health matters and contraception, nutrition, travel and vaccination, drugs and alcohol. Emergencies always receive priority treatment.

Care leavers

A care leaver is defined as a young person between the ages of 16 and 25 years who has been in the care of a local authority for a period of time.

Care leavers are entitled to ongoing support at university and every effort is made to accommodate their needs through:

- peer mentoring
- designated members of staff as first point of contact to offer support
- priority with accommodation
- priority with mental health counselling and services

Universities uphold the highest standards of confidentiality and will not share information without the student's consent.

Support centres

Universities run support centres to help students in certain areas within their particular course of study. These centres can provide assistance in many subjects such as: mathematics, science, computer programming and languages.

Many universities operate learning centres which can incorporate all of these kinds of support. Information regarding the use of information technology services and equipment is also provided.

You will need to establish from the outset what support services may be available to you in your chosen course of study.

Personal tutoring/mentoring/student advisory services

You have already been introduced to the personal tutoring system in Part I page 13 and earlier in this part on page 34.

Many universities now offer mentoring services. A mentor is a more experienced peer, usually a year or two ahead of you, who has volunteered and is trained to help new students settle into the university. They can provide you with information that is based on their experiences and is up to date, and they can answer questions about studying and socializing at the university. Some mentors organize social activities and bring groups together. Others can be contacted in person or online to answer specific questions. Mentors are a very useful resource. In due course you might consider becoming a mentor too.

Peer mentoring programmes to help first-year students settle into university are available in most universities. The mentors are students who are in their second or final year of their own university journey.

Mentors undergo training for this role and are generally matched with students from their own course or department. The aim is to provide new students with information and skills to ease their transition to university, to give them a sense of belonging and to ensure that they know where to find support and services. Some practical help can include a tour of the university campus, the various administrative and academic offices, convenient travel routes and some wise words on the 'dos and don'ts' in the first-year experience, both academically and socially.

Mentors enjoy the interaction with new students, and new students find this offers them an easy way to get involved in the university community.

If you have a concern, at any time, which is affecting your personal, social or academic development, try to seek out the help of the many professionals providing these services. It is important to remember that a problem shared is a problem halved.

All universities run a confidential tutoring/mentoring/student advisory system which is designed to provide support for all students. This is of particular importance for you to know as you make the transition from school to university. Tutors and advisors are there to provide you with direction on any matters relating to academic, practical, personal or social issues of concern. Your tutor will be sufficiently experienced to direct you to the appropriate administrative, academic or support service.

Often a short meeting with your tutor solves the problem in hand and can save you a lot of time and effort in the end. Your tutor can be the first point of contact; however, you are also free to make direct contact with any of the offices providing services.

Drawing on your personal resources

Making the university yours depends on how you engage and participate. This engagement has to be self-driven.

Be your own driver.

In summary:

- **Manage your learning process:** To be successful at university you need to be proactive and take ownership and responsibility for your own learning.
- **Believe in your ability:** Things will seem very strange at first. All students feel the same.
- **Take ownership and responsibility:** Find out the academic demands of your course early on. Be in control of your timetable.
- **Read the handbook:** Every course has one. Read it and read it often.
- **Start as you intend to continue:** Attend everything. Seek out all student services and supports that you need.
- **Develop a strong work ethic:** A consistent approach to your study works. Learn how to manage your time effectively, balancing different deadlines.
- **Be organized:** Date your lectures, take notes and rewrite your notes soon afterwards, and file them in an orderly manner for easy retrieval.
- **Back up your work:** Store this information in different and accessible places. A lost or blank memory stick at a presentation gathers no marks.
- **Get to know yourself better:** Understand your strengths and weaknesses; know when you are comfortable in situations and when you feel threatened. Remember there is help at your university. It is always good to talk.
- **Get involved:** University is not all about study – follow your interests.
- **Learn how to touch-type:** A little bit of training early on lasts a lifetime.
- **Make things happen:** Set your own goals, monitor your progress, seek feedback and be kind to yourself when things happen.

Concluding paragraphs

You have come from a school setting where you were communicated to frequently about assignments, payments, registrations, many of which could be overdue and simply resolved with covering notes and telephone calls from interested parents/guardians. This will not happen at university.

It is of vital importance that you have access to all facilities at the university and you will need to quickly establish with the academic registry services that you have been registered properly. The numbers attending your university are large. It is up to you to ensure that you are fully registered as a student in order to use all the services including computing, library, careers, health, academic services, student advisory services and more. If you are late with registration, you will be cut off from these services and reinstatement can attract fines and waste valuable learning time.

You are expected to be on time and to deliver according to the rules of your course. Heavy penalties are usually imposed for late delivery of coursework, which costs time, money and marks. Read the instructions very carefully for each set assignment and consult your handbook. You will need to read the rules and regulations frequently.

You should never assume that one set of rules applies to all assignments across all courses and disciplines. This is not the case and so it is important to read instructions carefully relating to all assignments at the appropriate time. Changes can and will be made to deliverables from time to time and this will be communicated to you. The responsibility lies with you to ensure that you pick up on any of these changes over the course of your studies.

Take responsibility for finding out deadline dates, examination and assessment times yourself. Many students find themselves turning up on the wrong day or at the wrong time because they heard the information through their peers. It is your responsibility to be satisfied that you have been informed about examination/assessment details by your university offices and not your peers.

Part III will explore the skills required at university to survive: how to make the most of study time, lecture time, team working and learning, research skills, academic writing, and a variety of other skills to ease your journey of discovery.

Troubleshooting section

Top tips
- Read the handbooks
- Be organized
- Get involved
- Stay connected
- Check emails
- Meet your tutor
- Create a support network

This could be you

I am struggling with lectures and the need to develop new skills
Seek out the academic support offering workshops in study skills, note-taking, team working and learning. Talk to your fellow students and find out what works well for them. Get in touch with your tutor, who can guide you to the most appropriate service to meet your needs.

I am falling behind in my studies
It is useful to write down why you are falling behind in your studies. What is getting in your way? Break the problem down into small achievable goals. Start today by making a plan for each day over the next week. Perseverance and consistency works. Talk to your tutor.

I know I will have to miss a lecture
It is almost impossible to attend everything. Inevitably life gets in the way and occasionally you may not be able to attend for your own personal reasons. Establishing connections with your peers early on in your course is recommended for many reasons. You will find a like-minded person with whom you can make an arrangement to take notes in either's absence and share and discuss them as soon as practicable after the missed lecture – a 'study buddy'.

It is important to establish if there is compulsory attendance required – this being the case you will need to make contact with the academic and/or course director to advise them of your intended absence and they will direct you accordingly.

I am overly anxious
The feeling of anxiety is a normal emotion and part of life's experience. However, sometimes this anxiety can become more intense and severe leading to persistent worry and an inability to function in everyday situations. Just like the problems with falling behind in studies, it is good to establish why you are overly anxious. Is this a personal or academic issue? It is important to talk to someone about your fears and worries. This could be a friend, a study buddy, a fellow student, your tutor or a member of the team of the university wellbeing/student advisory service.

I am having difficulty with the terminology
This is perfectly normal at this stage in your studies. Attend everything you can which might help you to understand the terminology used. Try to gather a few of your classmates together and work through the meanings and interpretations of the various terms used. Things will begin to settle half-way through the first semester.

International students

I just can't seem to fit in

Fitting in is one of the most challenging issues facing university students. Again, we have to ask why do you think you are not fitting in? Are you making an effort? Have you joined any clubs or societies? Clubs and societies attract students because of common interests not their country of origin. Find something new that interests you at your university.

If English is not your native language, have you been working on improving your skills? Talk to your tutor.

I am homesick

Weekends are particularly problematic for students who feel homesick and routines that complete the family week are very much missed. Try to organize a 'potluck' meal by inviting a group of students to get together and bring a favourite dish to share. This can be cheap and cheerful and great fun.

Other avenues to explore to combat homesickness might be to get involved in some local charity work in an area of special interest to you. The Students' Union office will have lists of the charities supported by students at your university. Another networking opportunity too! Talk to your tutor.

Building employability skills

- Use the first year to develop new academic skills and ways of learning, and these will contribute to your employability
- Understand the newer concept of tight and often conflicting academic deadlines at the university
- Work out a timetable and establish what resources you will need to meet these deadlines

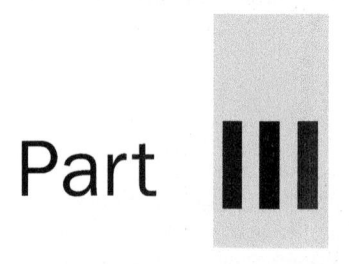

Part III
University Skills

Now that you have become more familiar with the structure of the academic year and the type of demands that it places on you, let's take a look at the typical set of skills that you will need to deliver to your deadlines and pave the road to academic success. There are many skills required, from the simple to the complex. The acquisition of these skills is an incremental process and takes time and practice.

The content in this section serves as an introduction to these skills. Your university will run workshops to guide you in greater detail regarding expectations. Increasingly the development of these skills is built into the core curriculum, while workshops are supplementary and should be used as appropriate.

In this section, we will look at the following:

- Studying to get results
- Setting goals
- Managing time effectively
- Team working and learning
- Study groups
- Thinking critically and analytically
- Preparing for lectures
- Making notes
- Study skills and memory
- Listening skills
- Research skills
- Academic writing skills
- Essay writing
- Assessment
- Referencing and plagiarism
- Going digital
- Communication and presentation skills

Studying to get results

The challenge of studying to get results rests with the learner. Managing your own learning by taking control and ownership of your learning journey will bring academic success. It is important to believe in your own ability and to be open to receiving constructive criticism from academics and peers to enable you to further your advancement in the discovery and application of knowledge through your course of study. To achieve this, you will enter into the realm of active learning, becoming the driver of your own success.

Adopt the company of positive people around you, which will help to build positive relationships, encouraging personal and professional growth while developing a sense of enquiry and furthering your zest for knowledge and discovery.

So what is success, we might ask?

Success is unique to each and every one of us and can be simply described as setting and achieving your own goals. What do you hope to achieve?

At university the setting of goals is your sole responsibility, quite different from your last experience of formal education. In the setting of your academic goals it is your duty to find out the academic demands of your course. Your handbook will guide you through this process.

Setting goals

Goals can be defined as short term, medium term and long term. What is important to note when defining goals is that they must be specific, realistic, set within a time frame, measurable and have a built-in review process. Having a reward built into the achievement of any goal can incentivize you to stick to the timelines. A reward can be little or large, but think of something that you enjoy and that's unique to you.

It might be useful to pause and write down your goals as you read through this section. The challenge of committing thought to document is a valuable exercise as it forces you to think through the various aspects of goal setting and how you might propose to achieve those goals.

Some questions that might assist you in this process:

- What is it you hope to do?
- Acknowledge the benefits to you/others?
- What barriers are in your way?
- Can you find a solution and overcome these barriers?
- Can you break down the solution into smaller parts?
- What resources can you call on?
- What time limits can you set for achieving your goal(s)?
- Is this achievable in the time limit set?

Set an action plan by defining the goal, setting time limits and describing action steps with a built-in review process. It's good to look forward to rewarding yourself for the achievement of the goal.

Action plan

Name the goal	Time limit	Action steps	Review	Reward	Comment

Managing time effectively

Have you ever given much thought to how you spend your time? The effective management of your time is an essential component in achieving set goals.

Do you make good use of your day or do you waste time? Time wasted is time gone. A little more thought into how you spend time might generate a new approach to your day.

We must sleep, eat, attend lectures and engage in various other activities both on and off campus, online and offline. We have to study, meet friends, fulfil family obligations, deal with emergencies and have some downtime. There is a lot to do but we must learn to prioritize in order of importance and urgency. It is essential to map out a realistic timetable to juggle what we have to do in order to establish how much time we can make available towards the achievement of any goals set.

When you are mapping out a time frame for setting and achieving your goals, it is useful to keep a calendar close to hand so that you can factor in events such as family celebrations which can change the course of your study patterns. Do you think that you could organize your time in a more effective way?

Let's take a look to see if you are guilty of time-wasting.

- Do you find yourself making excuses for unfinished work?
- Are you constantly putting things off?
- Are you always making excuses?

- Do you have a place for everything and have everything in its place?
- Do you put things back where they belong?
- Do you lose things a lot?
- Do you find yourself spending endless time looking for things?
- How organized is your workspace?
- Are you a 'Post-its' or a 'notebook' person?
- Do you move from task to task without completing any of them?
- Do you switch off your devices to avoid interruptions?
- Do you lie on in bed for hours thinking about what you have to do rather than 'doing'?
- Do you have little piles stacked everywhere but no idea what is in them?
- Are you a perfectionist – can you let something go?
- Are you always in crisis mode?
- Do you bother with 'to do' lists, or is that for others?
- Do you prioritize work?
- Do you factor in demands placed by family, special events, vacations and unforeseen events?
- Are you easily distracted?
- Are you a starter but not a finisher?

Try the Time-wasting challenge exercise to make a list of where your strengths and weaknesses lie in the various categories.

Time-wasting challenge

Here's what I am good at	Here's what I need help with

So often we hear ourselves saying '*if only things were different*'. It is important to understand that we only have the ability to change ourselves and what we do. We can only seek to manage the behaviour of others and try to influence them to make changes.

We can make things different by defining the change we want and by setting a goal that will help towards achieving this change. Habit plays a huge part in making these changes. There is widespread opinion on how long it takes to form habits, but this is dependent on many different factors, so there is no one size that fits all. However, it is acknowledged that 21 days upwards can break cycles of habit and lead to making new and well-formed habits.

If we look at something as simple as a 'to do' list and try to introduce this to your end-of-day routine over a three-week period, you will soon see that patterns emerge, and you will find yourself doing this on autopilot. You will be more than surprised at the benefits you will get from doing this exercise. Likewise, by incorporating a 30-minute walk every day as part of a daily routine for 21 consecutive days you will find that you will be eager to continue the practice thereafter.

Any plan is better than no plan, so it stands to reason that the setting of achievable goals has to bring some benefit, either short term or long term or both.

Team working and learning

Teams are essentially units of performance, united in the one goal with clear tasks and a common purpose. Working in teams is very beneficial when the team is performing well, but on the other hand where there is little cohesion, working together can be problematic. In some cases, you will be assigned to particular teams so you are placed in a situation where you have to make things work regardless of internal conflicts which may arise. In other cases, you are placed in a situation to self-select your team, which can present its own issues as you may not know others' working styles and you may also find that some students work in 'cliques' which have been obviously formed early on.

Team working is an essential employability skill, as in the work context you will generally not be in a position to select your team. Learning to work with others is vital.

When self-selection is required, you need to move quickly to find your team members. Within team working and learning there are diverse opinions and approaches, and inevitably individual students will be stronger and weaker in different aspects of the group assignments. This can result in both positive and negative experiences.

At the outset, it is important to establish the task you have been asked to complete and make sure that members have a clear understanding of their role and input to the project in hand. Rules acceptable to all members should be set at the first meeting and members reminded when necessary as the project develops. Start as you intend to continue. Every meeting should have a purpose, a plan and a process.

Different learning styles suit different people and some will be at different stages of development from you. Inevitably you will be part of a team in which there are underperforming members, or it may also be possible that you will be an underperforming member yourself. All input is required by members to achieve the end goal, but often the workload is not evenly spread and yet all team members get the same academic reward. Regardless of input, the work is presented as one final piece with each member receiving the same outcome in the academic assessment.

If underperformance by others becomes a major issue in your team, this has to be brought into the open amongst the members in the first instance and discussed to find a resolution. If this is not possible, you should make this known to the relevant academic lead. However, be prepared that the request may not be acted upon.

Your tutor will also be in a position to advise. While this experience is not welcomed by the proactive and committed student, it is worth noting that the practice at working in teams, regardless of performance, will stand you in good stead when attending for interview, and ultimately in the workforce where team working is an integral part of the skill set which employers seek.

There will be workshops available to you at your university to introduce you to the art of working in teams and in the formation of study groups.

Some questions you might have when placed in a team setting:

- Is there a natural leader in the team?
- How does this leader relate to the other members of the team?
- How will decisions be made?
- Who will make the rules?
- When, where and how will you meet?
- Are there clear expectations from each member of the team?
- If there is disagreement, how can these decisions be made?
- Can the team be changed?

Study groups

Study groups can be very beneficial. There is no set number, but somewhere between three and six people is ideal. They can take place anywhere – online or on campus or at some other suitable venue, which could be your residence or a nearby coffee shop or local hostelry.

It is important that the purpose of the group is clearly defined and ground rules are set from the beginning. Study groups may evolve naturally from allocated project groups or students may seek out other like-minded students to form such groups. Diversity in the group brings a critical and independent approach to thinking.

Study groups are normally self-selected. A word of caution if you are self-selecting: look for positive people, the 'can do' people. You will be amazed how motivated you can become and what you can discover about yourself, others and the subject(s) under discussion in a positive atmosphere. These groups help to boost self-confidence, increase depth of knowledge, and help members to keep focused on their studies and to keep on track with deadlines. Such groups also provide opportunities to draw on different opinions and perspectives and afford deeper engagement with areas that members may have a strong knowledge or interest in.

Some questions you might have starting out:

- Who are these other people?
- What am I expecting from them?
- What is expected from me?
- Where do I fit in?
- What's in it for me?
- Where are we headed and why?
- What are our goals?
- How much work and time will this involve?
- How can we continuously improve as members?

Study groups help you to address complex issues and to tease out opinion and argument, which increases conceptual understanding of topics under discussion. They also build a sense of belonging and commitment among the group members through information sharing and participation. They also provide a sound platform to disseminate information and solve problems. Joining a study group is a voluntary activity, unlike the team-working situation which is typically attached to a specific academic assignment or course of assignments.

Thinking critically and analytically

Independent learning is the art of taking control of your own learning. Moving to a world of self-directed independent learning at university exposes the mind to different styles and approaches, with an obvious shift in mindset from the regurgitation of facts on set material to an emphasis on understanding and critical thinking.

The transition to learning at university can be problematic for some. Fear of poor academic performance is a worry to the new student. These worries are easily resolved when the student becomes active rather than passive in the learning process.

At university you will learn how to learn and how to think critically and analytically. You will learn to actively seek out information and validation. You will also learn to delve deeply into the many facts and opinions expressed on a subject, and with the help of the academic community around you become adept at discerning the good from the bad and how to establish what is considered credible information. When you express an opinion you will become used to seeking out academic evidence to support or refute that opinion, and you will work towards reaching a position where you are capable of critically discussing and analysing conflicting opinions and drawing conclusions about the argument presented.

An intellectually curious mind is key to developing your critical and analytical thinking skills and creativity. The development of these skills gives the student motivation and confidence, and an awareness of their abilities, limitations and areas for growth.

Preparing for lectures

Make the best use of lecture time. Prepare where possible for your lectures. If you can, read in advance and question what you need to know. Whether using pen or keyboard, you need to be organized to get the most out of this time.

Date every lecture in your notes, giving each one a new page or section. Develop your own shorthand code. Identify verbal signposts that you may pick up from your lecturer indicating the importance and relevance of the subject under discussion. Note why these points are significant and when they might be most useful.

Almost every lecture will have a simple structure of a beginning, middle and an end. It is also equally important to read up on the topics covered at the lecture as quickly as possible afterwards.

Making the best use of notes

The art of good note-taking is an acquired skill, and an essential one to develop at university. Notes serve many purposes: they are good for summarizing; they link one lecture to another; and they will serve as quick revision of major issues raised at lectures or tutorials and other interactions at university.

Notes should be divided into different subject areas and clearly marked for easy retrieval.

Date your notes and keep them in chronological order. Listen for the roadmap for examinations and assignments, noting the emphasis the academics place on certain aspects of the course – if an academic states the obvious such as: 'note this down' or 'this is probably the most important part' or 'you will have an assignment based on this' or 'this argument is core to the development of this theory'.

Your notes are your personal guide in your study and should be rewritten as soon as possible after the individual lecture/interaction. This will aid memory, retention and retrieval and give you quick revision of the main issues. The information will be more easily retained if written up within the day of the note-taking while it is still fresh in your mind.

Your notes should reflect a summary of the lectures attended and link with other lectures following in the same subject area. These notes should be filed in a systematic order with clear divisions from other subjects. During the rewriting process, it is important to make use of supports that you might need to draw on such as: library, labs, tutorials, seminars, study group meetings and other university services.

Electronic files should always be backed up in more than one place. It is advisable to use a cloud-based solution and a robust external hard drive system. Using email to send work in progress is also a good habit to adopt. This applies to all your work. Excuses for lost material will not be accepted at university. It is your responsibility to ensure that your material is safe and retrievable at all times.

Study skills and memory

Getting down to studying can be difficult for many. A consistent approach is the key to success. Integral to study is the ability to access material easily so that it can be recalled it at relevant points during the academic course of study – be that at examinations or presentations, interviews or other situations, formal or informal. Such recollection depends on our ability to access information quickly.

The obvious questions include:

- Where can you study best – at university, at home, at your rented accommodation or other places?
- When is the best time for you to study? Is it late at night, early in the morning, at set times during the day or different times every day?
- How much time works for you to study best?
- Is your space organized?
- What time works best for you?
- Are you effective working for short or long periods?

No one size fits all. However, if you study over long periods, it is wise to take a break after 40–50 minutes to walk around, stretch your legs or have a glass of water.

It is important to have a question set out to answer for each study period. This gives a focus to the learning. Like all goals achieved, be kind to yourself with a treat when you have been effective during your study time.

As outlined earlier, group work can be beneficial to maximizing study opportunities and sharing information and opinions. Each student brings their own strengths and weaknesses to the table, some obvious and some not so obvious. Groups provide natural avenues to discuss assignments, difficult subject matter within the course, approaches to work and the introduction of new academic resources.

Memorizing material relies on a system of encoding, storage and retrieval: how we put in the information, how we store it and how we retrieve it. The simplest example of this is how we remember people's names. Have you ever struggled with this? Most people have and often we find ourselves encoding names through association, sometimes using distinct facial features or dress code or place association to help remember names.

You will have developed many ways of memorizing work in your previous experience in education. While the emphasis is not on rote learning at university, at times you will have to draw on a sound memory throughout the course of your studies and the various applications of your knowledge, be that in oral or in written settings. Revisit the goal setting section on page 57.

Students develop a variety of memory aids to help with memorizing material, which can include variations of acronyms, association of names and places, song and rhyme, lists in alphabetical or numerical order, codes, shapes and senses, among others. Mind maps are another useful visual tool to generate and represent ideas, helping to structure and analyse and ultimately to recall information. Mind maps can be written by hand or developed digitally using software.

The Roman Room system and the Loci (place) method are two ancient tools which were used to aid memory. You too can design your own room, mentally storing the items relating to the subject under study as you walk around that room – this offers you a visual way of recalling that information when required.

Bullet points are good aids to memory and will serve you well as you progress not only through your studies but also as you start your career journey. Think how you can elaborate on the various bullet points, noting how you might handle these in presentations when you are placed on the spot during question time. This can also act as a good gauge of how you might answer questions at examination time. Different subjects and questions require different approaches.

One-sheet summaries are also most valuable memory aids and should contain relevant and pertinent information about your subject. These summaries should be easy for you to see, follow and understand, and serve as quick revision to glean the major points relating to the subject or discipline under study.

When working on your memory, pay attention to your needs, use topic headings, summarize main ideas, establish links, find ways to check your learning and experiment using maps, charts, diagrams, acronyms and other methods to retain and retrieve information. Be comfortable and consistent with your application to study and how you allocate time and place to this important task.

Try to set up an organized place and a visible timetable. Eat something before you start and keep hydrated during your study sessions. Avoid interruptions, and if living with others make it known to them that you are in study mode. Personal distractions can cost you hours and sometimes days of study time. If you have fallen behind in your study, start the day as a new day. You can't turn the clock back, but you can make the most of the time ahead.

Find a system that works best for you.

Listening skills

Effective listening is a vital tool in your set of skills at university.

The good listener uses the ratio: 2:1. Two ears and one mouth, very like the old proverb associated with the tailor: 'measure twice and cut once'.

Effective listening works two ways. There is a responsibility on both the transmitter and the receiver of the information to ensure that the message can be understood. There is always some loss in the understanding of any message, as it is the listeners who ultimately interpret what they have heard. However, efforts can be made to engage with the speaker and give feedback – either verbal or non-verbal or both.

It is not unusual for your mind to wander when trying to listen to others, but try to consciously direct your attention to what is being said, and take some notes which will help you to concentrate. If you have difficulty understanding what is being said, then communicate this to the speaker at the earliest possible opportunity and before it causes embarrassment to you. If you have no interest in the subject matter or in hearing the speaker, then you might ask yourself why?

Generally poor listening occurs when there is little interest in the subject matter, listeners are preoccupied with unrelated thoughts, are distracted by extraneous noise, are tired or they simply can't hear what is being said.

University life fosters an environment conducive to effective listening, encouraging open-minded thinking, respecting different points of view and encouraging an atmosphere to support the interests and achievements of others.

Research skills

In Part II, 'Making it Your University', we broadly outlined the research process.

In the early stages of research, you need to know what is expected of you. Guidance is given at lectures and tutorials, and the library services will run workshops for this purpose. Useful questions include:

- What do I need to know?
- What are the time limits?
- How do I gather information?
- What resources will I need?
- Where can I go to find these resources?
- How will I document sources?
- How will I arrange my information?
- What referencing system will I use?
- How can I use information technology to my best advantage in this process?

When evaluating information:

- Is the author credible – how do I know?
- What am I being asked to believe?
- Is the argument valid and convincing?
- How accurate is it – what evidence is there?
- What have I learned?
- Where does this learning fit into my research question?

Over time you gather the information, then progress to evaluating it and within time begin to become a critical reader and thinker in the context of credibility of sources, academic argument and how this fits within your stage of learning. You will also develop the art of speed reading incrementally over time.

Academic writing skills

Academic writing can be described as a piece of writing on a specific subject aiming for academic achievement which makes sense to the reader, has a clear structure, presents points, reasons and opinion in a critical and analytical way and is supported by evidence of academic research.

Writing essays is the strongest example of how this writing applies at university. An essay is a complete piece of writing on a specific subject. It stands alone, makes sense to the reader, has structure, and leads us into an argument or discussion on a particular topic in an objective manner demonstrating evidence of research.

The title sets out the issue which needs to be addressed. The academic writer puts forward point, evidence, argument and opinion in a way which is clearly structured and leads the reader to a conclusion.

Academics grade these essays and in doing so look for the students' understanding of the subject and the key concepts, their power of expression and how they engage with the material in both an analytical and critical manner.

In considering the writing task set, you will need to determine the purpose of the writing, who will be reading and examining it, what essential information will be required to achieve different grades and how you will present that material.

Regardless of the length or the nature of the writing assignment, the writing stages comprise five distinct parts:

- Planning
- Drafting
- Editing
- Formatting
- Proofreading

Planning

In this part of the process, you need to know exactly who the audience is. Is this assignment set purely as a formal piece of academic writing to be examined by a member of the academic team or is it a peer-reviewed assignment? Is it a submission for a scholarship? Or is it a communication with a related industry which forms an integral part of your assessment?

It is important to match your output to the purpose of the assignment. Read and reread the instruction carefully. Think about the action or reaction your reader might make to this work and its presentation.

Familiarize yourself with the marking criteria for this assignment and keep that uppermost in your mind as you think through the planning stage. Record everything in narrative form that you include in your planning stage. This might surprise you, but you may use a lot of this information in the final draft.

Relevant content is key to the success of any academic endeavour. What content do you need to include as a basic requirement and what will make it stand out from the other submissions? There will be times in your university life when, regardless of ambition, you may have to settle for less than perfect submissions due to time constraints and conflicting timetables.

A useful set of questions to guide you in the information you present is:

- What information do you need to include in this piece of writing to get your message across?
- What must you include?
- What should you include?
- What could you include?

This is the time for brainstorming, the free association of ideas. Another useful tool in this part of the process is mind mapping. This visual method facilitates free thinking and a flexible approach.

In what order will you discuss the topic?

The organization of your content is critical. Group related ideas and identify which are major and minor points. Not all points receive equal emphasis. It is equally important to find academic evidence to support your points. Each major point presented will need reason, evidence and independent opinion. Your university will help you to understand this process by way of practical workshops.

No section on academic writing would be complete without addressing 'writer's block'. Academic, fiction, non-fiction writers, all writers suffer from it and you too will experience it from time to time. We have all been in the situation where you would do just about anything except get down to work when there is a 5000-word essay or a detailed report to be written. Even the most accomplished of writers find there are days when they just can't write or can't find the motivation or the stimulus to do so. Be patient and it will come.

Planning your work will help you overcome writer's block, as will the exercises of brainstorming and mind mapping. The freedom of committing thought to document is liberating in itself as the fear of writing irrelevant material can often become a barrier. You must remember that you are not alone if you feel you are writing irrelevant material. Every student has thoughts like this at many points during the course of their studies, but once the rough writing process begins, this dissipates.

Sometimes students consider formatting the document at an early stage as it helps them to focus and give the material structure, which in turn helps them to progress in the planning of the work. Please see the section on formatting on page 71. In time, through trial and error, you will find the system which suits you best.

Drafting

Your first draft is a gentle introduction to the project in hand and it is important that you stay in author mode. Engaging in idea generation and free writing around these ideas starts the process. This explorative work not only gives you confidence to keep going but speeds up your engagement with the material. Don't seek or expect perfection at this early stage. You can save that until the much later stages of the project. You will produce many drafts and the temptation to dismiss or discard them is great. Keep these drafts as different versions until you have completed the assignment in full. Very often, early material proves to be most useful in the final stages of reviewing and editing work.

Neither should you concern yourself with the mechanics or style of the work in your early drafts. By this we mean spelling, sentence structure, grammar, punctuation, word expressions, number expressions or word divisions. This will come later.

The reader in this case is your examiner, who is not looking for anecdotal accounts of life's experience but more specifically is looking for concrete content with sound argument using words and language that have definite meaning and relevance to the topic under discussion. Above all, your writing has to have the academic rigour of evidence of research. While you will need to adhere strictly to word counts set in particular assignments, it is important not to fill word counts by including material which is irrelevant and of poor quality. Unsupported assertions – that is, stating facts without any academic evidence to support them – is unacceptable.

It is useful to have a bank of action verbs to draw from which can describe different ways of saying similar things, such as:

- advance
- affirm
- agree
- articulate
- assert
- concur

- define
- express
- outline
- pose
- posit
- propose
- put forward
- report
- state

A good thesaurus and dictionary are essential tools for this purpose.

Editing

At this stage of the process you will move into writing with style, looking towards the overall writing tone, how effective it is, appropriate word use, how sentences are formed, how you use paragraphs and if they flow logically.

You will also be looking at how the writing conforms to standard language conventions and how your document is referenced academically. Check for unsupported assertions.

Editing is an iterative process where several readings and amendments are made to improve the quality of the work. The courteous and sincere tone of the work is important regardless of content or opinion. This overall style should take shape during each editing iteration.

When writing paragraphs, keep to one idea which can be introduced in the first sentence and supported by units of information in the following sentences to support it. Paragraphs should link between the preceding and following ones and lead the reader in a logical sequence. Try to keep your sentences short and make sure that the reader can make sense of the text.

Some things to note:

- Don't use language that discriminates on the basis of gender, race, sexual orientation, age, beliefs or religion
- Avoid words and phrases that imply gender except where it is relevant to the subject under discussion
- Avoid stereotypical terms
- Avoid clichés, slang and buzz words
- Avoid redundancies such as: 'combined together' and 'past history' – these can be written as just 'combined' and 'history' – and any unnecessary repetition of ideas or words

Checking for correctness and accuracy is essential at this stage, and includes grammar, style, syntax, word usage, punctuation and spelling. Such errors will distract your reader and cause misunderstandings. You are also checking for correctness in terminology and referencing of academic work. Please do not rely on the spellcheck function to help you in the editing task.

Formatting

The formatting stage looks at the presentation of the document and how it conforms to the formatting requirements attaching to the assignment set, incorporating layout, word count, spacing, margins, binding etc. The level of detail required will vary from assignment to assignment. If you have been asked to adhere to certain requirements, then failure to do so will cost you marks. On the other hand, marks can be easily gained by complying with the formatting requirements.

The formatting process may be incorporated into the planning stage, particularly if there are complex instructions. In some situations it is easier to format at the end, but some writers prefer to start the formatting process earlier. It is an individual approach.

Only accept the best standards from yourself regarding formatting of content. Read the instructions carefully and stick to them.

The instructions around formatting are generally clearly set out and very easy to follow. Certain styles will be requested and certain rules will pertain to the presentation of the document, whether that is in soft or hard copy or both.

Proofreading

The proofreading stage is about quality control. It is the time to review the document to check for content, flow, and typographical and formatting errors.

Proofreading happens after both major and minor revisions have been made. Superficial errors which are usually related to grammar, punctuation, spelling and the correct labelling of figures and tables are picked up at this stage. While most of the changes will have been made at the editing stage, this is the final opportunity to make the piece of work flow consistently in an organized manner, making it easier to read through and comprehend. It is important to cross-check titles, headings and subheadings with the table of contents, particularly in larger pieces of work. You will need to set aside some quiet time to complete this process. The length of time will be dependent on the volume and type of work involved.

When the subject of academic writing is under discussion, the dreaded apostrophe and its use – not to mention its misuse – needs to be addressed. Take time to research its correct use in the English language. Once learned, you will never forget it.

The time that you will give to each of the these five steps depends on the length and importance of the document, its complexity and its worth and value to you in the context of academic grading of the subject and how that affects the grade in your overall discipline. They are vital steps and a sound platform for writing any academic assignments while at university. Such practices stay with you and will in turn prove beneficial in your working life.

Essay writing

One of the typical assignments set during your time in university involves essay writing. Essays provide opportunities for you to deepen your learning using research and ideas conforming to the rigours of academic writing. They are a core part of assessment of your learning on a particular subject or topic area, and will have set word lengths and strict formatting instructions and clear marking criteria.

Some make many common mistakes with their first essays. Many write to a high standard on the set topic but fail to answer the question asked. They often become overambitious in what they think they can achieve, by doing too much research and presenting an argument that is hard to follow.

In these early stages of work, structure is often weak with an inappropriate tone and writing style which is presented poorly and with academic texts and quotations not correctly referenced.

Some questions to ask yourself before you submit your essays:

- Have you answered the question posed?
- Have you covered the main points in the topic? Think about the 'musts', 'shoulds' and 'coulds' in this section.
- Are these main points supported by academic evidence?
- Are your academic sources properly referenced in the text and in your reference list?
- Is your content relevant and accurate?
- Is there a link from paragraph to paragraph, presented in a logical sequence?
- Are you bringing the reader from a sound introduction to the set topic, signposting the direction of the essay through to the main body and argument, and finishing with a strong summary in the conclusion?
- Have you adhered to the requested formatting style?
- Have you made a back-up copy of your work?

Simply put, essays need structure: has this work got an introduction, a main body/development and a conclusion?

Assessment

You will be assessed on your academic progress in different ways. Assessment takes many forms, from the traditional examination hall setting to continuous assessment by coursework, online submissions, multiple choice questions, fieldwork, demonstrations and a variety of oral presentations.

The principal purpose of the examination and assessment process is to ensure that understanding of what is being taught is achieved, that academic standards are upheld and that evidence of learning to standards set by the university is demonstrated by the students. The continuous processes and the variety of these processes serve as a good barometer of students' progress, providing academic feedback to develop further potential.

Examinations are opportunities for students to demonstrate their understanding of what they have learned, and this is what examiners will look for. When you start an assignment, whether online or offline, in informal or formal settings, you start with zero marks but build marks with every piece of relevant information you provide in answering the problem that is presented to you.

However, many students associate examinations with stress and often have nightmares about them. Anxiety builds up as we worry more, just like other fears such as the fear of finding a spider in the shower, fear of public speaking and fear of flying or heights. These fears may relate to fear of failure, rejection, past experiences or fear of the consequences of failure. These anxieties need to be managed.

In order to do that we need to take control. Examinations are like a train journey – there are many stops on the way. They are not just about the final drop-off point. Increasingly universities are looking at ways to move away from the formal examination model and setting more coursework assignments to bridge this gap.

Ultimately, it's that fear of failure that takes over at examinations and tugs at your confidence and transfers to your ability to perform.

So, let's look at why might you fail an examination:

- You turn up on the wrong day. Your responsibility is to find out when and where and how examinations will take place. Do not depend on fellow students to inform you of these dates and times or the rescheduling of any examinations. Things change quickly at university for a variety of reasons. Check your university email account every day for notices of changes and refer to handbooks and noticeboards. Be sure that you are clear how the university will communicate such changes and take responsibility for finding out this information.
- You haven't prepared. The answer here is obvious. Poor preparation leads to poor performance. It is up to you to ensure that you adequately prepare.
- You haven't read the question properly. Read the question; read it again and again.
- You are answering the wrong question. As above, read the question, underline the key points and refer back to these points at intervals to ensure you are on track.
- You are not reading the instructions. Read and read again and underline the key instructions. Perhaps you were asked to answer three out of five questions but didn't notice that question 1 was compulsory? Did you miss the last part of the instruction?
- Your presentation is poor and hard to follow. While this is understandable in formal examination situations, you would be expected to present material such as continuous assessment coursework and oral presentations in a clear

and fluid manner. Think about your introduction, development and conclusion and how they flow and link into each other – a simple but effective model. In formal written examinations, leave blank spaces after each question as you may wish to return to add in further information during the sitting.

- You are not recognizing the key issues. Read the question; read it again and read it again.
- You get a feeling of panic that you know nothing, that you can't answer anything. Stay calm. Breathe deeply – use the brainstorming technique to draw out information relating to the subject and then build your answer around that information.
- You are becoming personal about the situation. In your mind, put the question in the middle of the table and ask yourself: if you were working in a study group, how might you approach an answer to this question?
- 'I can't remember a thing' is a common reaction. The more we convince ourselves that our memories are poor then the poorer our memories will become. Think positively and calmly. If you have put in the work, the rest will follow. This is the time when those bullet points and summary sheets, discussed in the 'Study skills and memory' section (on page 64), are lifesavers.
- You leave early. When in the formal examination hall or on a time limit to deliver online, avoid the temptation to leave early; inspiration often comes in those last minutes.
- You worry afterwards about what everyone else has done. Ignore the voices of others. Once assignments are delivered and examinations are over, they are over. No benefit will be gained by exchanging with fellow students on what you submitted and what you may have omitted (with good reason). This type of post-mortem only serves to lower your confidence and set you on a wrong footing when tackling your next examinable component. Have confidence in your own ability. This journey is about you, not about your fellow students.
- You run out of time. Attempt that last question and use bullet points to demonstrate that you are familiar with the main concepts which you would have addressed had you had more time. You will get marks for this attempt, provided there is relevance to the question being asked. Again, the practice of using summary sheets and bullet points as memory aids is invaluable at this critical time.

Referencing and plagiarism

The art of referencing correctly is at the heart of all academic writing and is an integral part of the university system. You will be formally introduced to this system during your first weeks at the university when it will be explained and demonstrated for your benefit.

Workshops on how to reference material appropriately are widely available across all universities. Referencing material in this way guards against the academic offence of plagiarism.

Committing an offence of plagiarism means that you are claiming to be the author of work that is taken directly from a source without acknowledging the source's origins and/or authors. You will need to carefully examine how you seek out information and how you seek validation for such information as well as how you document your sources.

You must acknowledge your sources of information. Taking good notes in the course of your research will save time in completing the many reference lists associated with your assignments. There is a strict system of referencing imposed at each university, and the system of choice at your university will be the one you will use throughout the course of your study there.

You will need to familiarize yourself with the rules and regulations around plagiarism, which will be very clearly explained by way of an information booklet and/or specific training run by the library or the academic counselling services. Digital solutions are employed to promote academic integrity and detect plagiarism.

The breaching of referencing protocols is very much frowned upon at university and such breaches carry severe penalties, up to and including expulsion from your course or university.

Going digital

Online learning platforms are integral to the university systems and support. They provide many details about the course contents, assessment resources etc., and are gateways to address a wide range of issues. Library services such as online databases are typical resources found at any university today.

The pandemic of 2020–21 has moved more teaching online across the world, creating challenges for both staff and students in terms of delivery and attendance. Zoom, Google, Apple, Microsoft Teams etc. facilitate much of this delivery. It can be more difficult to engage in this learning environment, and it can be tempting to log in but not attend. Actively engaging through exercises, breakout groups, listening, note-taking, asking questions and posting comments are important to your learning and to the development of a healthy online learning community.

Technology is playing an increasing part in the production and dissemination of information and in particular fast-forwarding research, which results in the compilation and publication of vast quantities of academic papers and journals. This output is growing at an exponential rate and proving challenging for students in discerning what is most relevant and credible in the context of their own studies. The library services will run workshops to assist you to do this.

'Digital' encompasses everything to do with how technology is applied to education, how students engage with it and how it is used as a tool to drive performance in a world that by its very progress in technology is imposing unprecedented change on our planet in the way we work and live.

Most students will have their own technological equipment, but many students will depend on high-performing computing machines to carry out practical work and high-level research, depending on the discipline under study. Universities invest significant monies each year installing and updating sophisticated equipment for this purpose.

A lot of investment is made in developing innovative ways of teaching and learning in the digital age. As a learner, you will need to embrace the change that the digital era brings across all that you engage in at university. In the use of technology there will be a code of conduct expected and breaches of that conduct will, like plagiarism, bring severe penalties. Software systems such as Turnitin are used to check for these breaches.

It is important to respect the facilities that are offered to you. You shouldn't share passwords with others or allow peers or friends access to your university digital space. It is good practice to change your passwords frequently and to ensure that security is up to date on all the equipment you use. Like all shared equipment, please leave the equipment in the manner you would like to find it and try to share the time spent on the higher performing machines with your fellow students. If you notice that any machine might be posing a security threat, you are obliged to make contact with the appropriate support office at your university.

When using online platforms in the course of your studies or as any part of course delivery, a polite code of conduct is expected through this medium. Regardless of the medium used, online or face to face, equal respect should be given. Likewise, the use of email, social media and any other communication bearing the university name should conform to the same polite code of conduct.

You need to familiarize yourself with the rules surrounding the use of technology at your university. Your handbook and information technology support office will guide you in all of these matters.

Students have access to a wide range of hardware and software solutions and online services at discounted prices through the information systems services at the university. Make contact with the Students' Union to find out more about these.

Communication and presentation skills

Communication and presentation skills are interconnected; however, they are often looked at as two quite separate and distinct operations. Communication can be simply expressed as the sharing of ideas or information, a process through which messages can be sent or received. Above all, communication is a two-way interactive process. Similarly, it is natural that presentation should fall in the same category. However, we must ask ourselves the questions: Are we communicating? How are we communicating? How do we know the communication is effective and is it a two-way process? If not, why not? Why make a presentation at all?

During your years at university you will be tasked with a variety of ways to present your academic findings and express your academic opinion. Many of these will take the form of a formal presentation and many automatically assume that PowerPoint is the only answer. We are all familiar with the expression 'death by PowerPoint' which often puts the audience to sleep, and particularly where the presenter reads the material directly from the slides in a bid to gain the full attention of the audience. Slides presented should be designed for the benefit of your audience, with minimum information displayed, only acting as a prompt for the person delivering.

Given that fear of speaking in public is top of the list of the major stressors in life, it's not surprising that many presenters fall short of making the most of these opportunities and are filled with dread in anticipation of brain freeze during the process. So how can we build confidence in how we communicate in these situations?

Let's have a look at a formal presentation in which you need to communicate effectively, regardless of the medium used. Presenting formally will form an integral part of your experience during your studies and future careers. If you have a fear of speaking in public, now is the time to tackle it.

Effective presentation and communication can be simply divided into three distinct stages:

- Preparation
- Practice
- Presentation

Preparation

The preparation stage comprises four distinct parts:

- Audience
  To whom are you speaking?
- Subject
  What information are you delivering?
- Method
  How will you deliver that information?
- Self
  How well are you prepared?

Audience

The audience is your responsibility: you are going to share your information with them, so you have the control. You need to find out more about them.

Who is in that audience? Why are they attending? What do they know about you? What do you know about them? What assumptions are you making? What do they know about the topic already and what do they need to know?

Have you taken time to consider the audience age group? How can you deal with the cross section of age and experience within the audience? Are you presenting to fellow students, to societies, to an academic, to university committees, to study groups, for examination, in a competition or maybe to industry? How will the subject matter differ with each of these audiences?

If you are addressing a multicultural audience, it is important that you know this and understand the many cultural differences that exist. This will be covered in more detail in the 'Culture and diversity' section in Part IV. What is acceptable in one culture may be considered rude or insulting in another. It's always better to find this out before you begin.

Communicating with a variety of people imposes different demands. How many are you expecting to attend? Are you presenting to 2, 10, 20, 50 or 100 people? Your approach will differ depending on the anticipated number. You must also be prepared to adjust your delivery if the expected larger numbers do not attend, which can throw many presenters.

Subject

What does your audience know about the subject? Are they your examiners? If so, what are they expecting from you? What is the purpose of the presentation? What is their attitude to you and the subject? What is your attitude to them and the subject? What key information do you need to get across?

Identify the 'musts', 'shoulds' and 'coulds' in that order. What must I include in this presentation? What should I include? What could I include? If this is an academic exercise, think about the criteria set for the grading. Separate your 'musts', 'shoulds' and 'coulds' into three separate piles, and think about how they interrelate and how relevant each is to the subject in hand. Imagine travelling abroad and what you might pack into a carry-on suitcase on the aeroplane. Do you need to bring everything with you? The simple answer is no. What you bring with you will need to be useful.

What must you include to make this presentation successful? If it is an academic assignment, what criteria have been set to achieve a certain grade? What is the minimum you need to provide? What 'should' be included if this work is to get good marks, and lastly what could you include to make it stand out from the rest and impress?

Avoid slang, clichés and jokes, and be respectful of age and cultural differences. Understand the environment in which your presentation is taking place.

Method

A sound structure leads the audience in a systematic way from start to finish in a simple three-part model of a beginning, middle and end.

Feedback is important. Listen and read the audience as you speak. How can you be sure that your audience is engaging? How can you make it interesting enough that they don't fall asleep or spend most of the time checking phones or doodling? If that happens, how will you handle that?

Clarity in presentation is crucial to bring understanding, to unify thoughts and ideas, to break down complex issues to emphasize the level of importance.

An effective communicator can anticipate most of the questions that might be asked. However, in the world of academia, even the most accomplished presenters will be taken by surprise.

If you are unsure of what is being asked, say so and ask the person to repeat the question. In turn, repeat what you think has been asked to avoid ambiguity. Keep your answers to the point. If there are too many questions, this could mean two things: a) that the interest is great, and your presentation is fascinating or b) that you left out a lot of the most significant issues. Ask yourself which it is and why. This analysis of performance will serve you well as you develop this skill over time. If you get a blank, don't worry; this is much more common than you might think. Many presenters get blanks. This is where notes come in handy.

Notes are your personal guide to your work, and you should have them close to hand at all times during presentations or public speeches. Think about the many politicians and newsreaders and how much they rely on notes and make their own notes as journalists throw questions at them. Your notes are there to assist you, to keep you on track, but are not to be read word for word. Keep them close to you, with text on one side of the page only, with page numbers clearly visible to you and some pointers to remind you of the key elements of the subject under discussion.

Avoid multiple apologies if you lose your way. Root your feet firmly into the ground to regain your composure and seek assistance from your audience, if necessary, to get you back on track. In general, audiences are wishing you well too.

Self

Confidence plays a core part in effective communication. Confidence comes from knowledge, belief, control and practice: knowledge about self and material, belief in self and material, control of what you say and do, and lots of practice. Like the athlete heading for the winning line, we need to visualize success in order to share our ideas and information with the audience.

Practice

This is key to success especially when you are new to making presentations. Back up your work to the cloud and to external hard drives, and send an email with a copy of the presentation to yourself.

So many good points are lost in transit due to mumbling or speaking too quickly. Clarity in speech comes from good attention to the consonant sounds in our words. Consonants frame speech and vowels give them their sounds, their flow and their beauty.

You will need to practise your presentations. The bathroom is the best place to practise, in front of a big mirror where the acoustics are good. Practising in front of a mirror will make you slow down your speech naturally. You will also get used to the sound of your own voice. Lots of practice in your early days of formal presentation brings confidence. All that said, it is also important that you don't overdo the practice as then the delivery comes across as being forced, unnatural and uninteresting.

Presentation

Keep things simple. Explain what you are going to talk about, talk about it and then recap on what you have said. Let them know from the outset what they can expect. Have a clear questioning policy at the start. Will that be during or at the end of the presentation? Most of what we say is through our body language. You need to be enthusiastic and committed to your subject. You need to own it. Otherwise, how can you persuade your audience to buy into the concept and your approach?

A well-prepared presentation is obvious to all who see or hear it. It also helps calm the nerves. Regardless of how nervous you might feel, consuming alcohol or other substances before a presentation is a bad idea. If this is your practice, you will need to address that without delay and trust in your own ability and challenge yourself to be satisfied that you are fit and able to communicate without any substances to assist. Avoid drinking tea or coffee as these are diuretics and you may end up having to excuse yourself at the wrong moment!

Take bottled water (still not sparkling) with you in case you need to take a drink during the presentation. If you use bottled water, there is less chance of having a major spill on your hands which would compound your nerves and take the attention away from the most important matter, the presentation of your hard work and material.

Face the fear and overcome it.

Confidence comes from knowing that you have taken the time to prepare well. In turn, this preparation will give you the self-belief that you need. This applies equally to both online and offline experiences.

Concluding paragraphs

In this section we have presented a set of core skills that you will develop and draw on over your time at university. In acquiring these skills, you will be prepared for the expectations that will be placed on you and develop confidence to approach tasks in a meaningful way. The management of time and your organizational skills will greatly contribute to this confidence building. Spend time working at each of the skills elaborated on in this section and try to incorporate goal setting into your study routines.

Good preparation for all tasks in hand will bring reward and facilitate the freedom to engage critically and analytically with theories and knowledge.

This planning and engagement results in the coherent presentation and discussion of sound argument and opinion, which in turn demonstrates your ability to deal with the expectations placed on you. Much discussion has also been given to the examination process which might help you in coping with what can be a very stressful situation for many students.

Part IV will look at health, identity and society and how these influence the student attending university.

Troubleshooting section

Top tips

- Use the first year in particular to develop new academic skills and nurture good habits
- Don't be afraid to seek help and guidance from peers, tutors, academic staff and student services
- Read assignment briefs fully and frequently

This could be you

I'm not getting the grades I want

At school you may have been used to getting top grades but at university you may not be achieving the same results. Seek out feedback from your lecturers on all work you've submitted to try to establish how you fall short in your expected results. Forming study groups with your peers to discuss assignments can be very beneficial. Mentors have already gone through this process and may be able to guide you. Once you understand why your grades are low, you can seek out the services to help you achieve better results. Talk to your tutor.

I feel overwhelmed by the academic demands on me

Most students feel just like you during the first semester in particular when everything is so new. Find out what help is available to help you overcome your fears. Workshops will be on offer on essay writing, presentation skills, research and study skills. Try to identify a few key areas that you are finding difficulty with, prioritize them and seek out appropriate help from the relevant university support services.

Talk to your tutor and/or some of your peers to see how they are getting on. You might be surprised at the tips they can give you. If possible, try to find a student in the year ahead who has been through a similar experience.

International students

Studying is taking a long time

This might arise for many reasons: your learning style; difficulties relating to culture and language; difficulty settling into new schedules and different writing styles. Allow yourself time to settle in. Try to give more attention to one particular aspect of your academic duties each week – for example, try giving extra time to understanding your lectures. If this is an issue for you, then study time will be difficult for you. Try to get help from your fellow students by discussing the lecture topics. Attend any workshops that are run specifically to help you with study skills, note-taking and academic writing. All of these will help your focus during your study sessions.

I am struggling with my English

This is very common with international students for whom English is a second language. To become proficient in a second language in order to carry out academic assignments at a high standard is particularly difficult. It also takes time to get used to dialects and accents.

Attend all workshops made available to you and seek out any special assistance you can get with the English language. It will take time to become proficient in the language and it can be more than frustrating at times when you feel you should be making more progress. Consistent communication with your peers using English is necessary. Read, write and listen to podcasts in English. Try to extend your network through attendance at student events, through societies and clubs and by speaking only in English. It is really important not to socialize exclusively with others who speak your mother tongue.

Listen to local and world news daily in English and listen to the same bulletins being delivered several times over the same day. Gradually you will become more confident with the sounds and the complex structure of the language. The rest will follow.

Building employability skills

The majority of the skills discussed in this chapter will be useful in the world of work, so cultivating skills now will contribute to your employability.

Start engaging with work-related opportunities, such as volunteering or a work shadowing scheme during your first year.

Work on your communication and team-working skills. These are key skills in the workforce today.

Part IV

Health, Identity and Society

This part of the book deals with health, identity and society and will be very useful in raising your self-awareness and engaging you to take control of all aspects of your life and your overall well-being. University education is not just about your academic experience, it's a preparation for another chapter in life's journey, in an ever-changing world.

In this part, we look at culture and diversity, gender and identity, together with looking after your physical, mental, emotional and spiritual self. We also explore the area of interpersonal communication. The issues of suicide, substance abuse, sleep health and anxiety are also addressed. A series of exercises complements this section. Students are encouraged to complete these exercises which establish strengths and gaps in both personal and professional growth. Once these strengths and gaps are identified, students are encouraged to set goals, which in time develops resilience, a skill which is key to dealing with the unexpected challenges which arise during the university experience and far beyond.

Within the umbrella of health, identity and society we will address the following:

- Culture and diversity
- Gender and identity
- Sexual consent
- Travelling and studying abroad
- Looking after yourself
  - Sleep patterns
  - Setting goals
  - Physical well-being
  - Mental well-being
  - Emotional well-being
  - Spiritual well-being
  - Interpersonal communication

- Suicide
- Anxiety
- Substance use and abuse
- Developing resilience
- Seeking help

Culture and diversity

The student body attending any university is diverse. The strong internationalization of the student population and the variety of countries it represents does not in itself create a common culture. What we see on the outside is not culture, neither does where we come from define our culture. It is how we understand and interpret others and their opinions and expressions that defines our culture.

The commonality of culture is highly dependent on the adaptation of students towards customs, beliefs, values, opinions and expressions which are based on how we view the world in our own culture. The exposure to the many cultures represented at your university develops an enquiring mind to establish different patterns and knowledge. It provides a safe platform to explore how others think and see things. There are many ways to solve problems; the challenge is to find the one that is most appropriate and effective and transferable across cultures. A quiet reflection of what culture means to you is useful to explore.

When you work in groups, you will find that different cultures approach problems in different ways. This challenges, forms and reforms relationships and sets the seeds for growth in relationships across cultures, understanding diversity across global borders. The nature of world commerce, immigration and globalization forces such growth and development.

How we communicate varies from culture to culture. The use of humour, for example, might be more dominant in the English culture, but how is that interpreted by other cultures? How verbal or non-verbal is our communication? Do we make eye contact? Do we touch? Do we observe personal space?

There are many other aspects to culture including language, dress, food and architectural landscapes. We make assumptions about what, when, where and how people cook and eat. We make assumptions about how people spend their time and what is considered to be high priority in one culture over another. We make these assumptions based on our own cultures and where we come from.

Sometimes it is perceived that those speaking the same language have the same cultures. If we look at cultures across the United Kingdom, we can see different opinion and expression and customs across Scotland, Wales, England and Northern Ireland. We can see the same between Spain and Latin America; France, DR Congo and Canada; America and Australia; Russia and Kazakhstan; China and Singapore.

According to the Equality and Human Rights Commission, universities must not unlawfully discriminate against their students. Hence any student who feels that he or she is being unfairly disadvantaged on grounds of age, disability, pregnancy, race (including colour, nationality, ethnic origin, national origin), sex, sexual orientation, gender reassignment, religion or beliefs should raise this matter with the Students' Union, tutors and/or counselling services at the university or the UK Equality Advisory & Support Office. Students also have the right to lodge a complaint under the Equality Act.

How can your cultural differences affect your interactions with others? Get involved in the broad range of clubs and societies offered at your university and enjoy the many enriching, diverse cultural experiences.

In essence, we must be aware of other cultures, respect these cultures, be cognizant of obvious and not so obvious differences, and seek to work together to develop a mutually agreeable way of working towards a positive outcome.

Cultural exchanges broaden the mind. Embrace them.

Gender and identity

Gender and identity are concerned with biological and psychological make-up and the influences under which we live in society. Family, friends and social media can place demands to behave in certain ways, conforming to social rules which may or may not be agreeable to you. While gender identity is generally defined at birth and is used on all formal identification papers and official documents, this defined birth gender can and may change over time.

Gender identity and expression encompasses male and female and transgender. Transgender is nothing new in society, with many references to be found historically across continents and cultures. What is different now is the freedom to express yourself through your own individual identity.

When we fall into the traditional male/female gender categories, few question why this is so, but those who are transgender are often questioned and judged. What is new to our society is the open acceptance of this individuality.

If you feel that you are struggling with your gender, identity and sexuality, seek out help through the many student advisory services available including; health, welfare, and wellbeing. The Students' Union provides a supportive environment. This is key to feeling positive about yourself and having a sense of belonging.

Sexual consent

It is important to know that sexual activity without consent is against the law. Consent is agreeing by choice because you want to, not because you are being forced to. Consent can be withdrawn at any time.

You shouldn't feel threatened or intimidated or coerced into making a decision. Intimidation may occur when there is a power imbalance or where there is a perceived 'hold' over you by the perpetrator.

Nobody has a right to do anything you don't want them to do to your body. If you agree to one thing, this does not mean you have implicitly agreed to more. Likewise, you have no right to do anything to anybody else's body without their consent. No means no.

Consent cannot be given when someone is:

- drunk or drugged
- under the legal age, which is 16 in England
- unconscious or asleep

If you have been the victim of a sexual assault, also seek out the assistance of the university services who will know what to do, who to contact, your rights and the support you are entitled to.

If you feel you have been or are being affected by any of the above, seek out support at your university through the counselling and health services.

Travelling and studying abroad

Many opportunities are afforded to students to study abroad during their time at university, which can prove to be an enriching and rewarding experience.

Travelling to another country to study, conduct research or spend time on work placements can be an integral part of your study programme. Such placements can be offered for a number of months or for the full academic year. Students also often travel during the summer months to find work or develop an appreciation of other cultures and improve their foreign language learning.

If your studies bring you to countries outside the UK on study abroad programmes or work placements, you must make sure you know the age of consent in that particular country. It is equally important to understand the law in relation to drinking alcohol, legal and illegal substance use (which can include painkillers), driving laws etc.

No matter where you live or travel to, the law is the law. It is your responsibility to understand it.

When making your plans, check that your passport is in date and all relevant visas are obtained and in order. Many countries insist that your passport must be in date for six months after your planned return date.

Finding accommodation abroad will be different in every country. Securing accommodation in a timely manner is advised. If you know where you are going and the duration of your stay, start looking early. If your placement is connected with your course, generally there is a coordinator appointed to deal with these placements. However, the responsibility lies with you to do your research. What kind of accommodation is on offer? Who will you be sharing with? Where is the accommodation? Is it near the campus? Sometimes the campus may be geographically positioned far from where the action happens at night or at the weekends. Safety should be high on your priority list.

All rent agreements should be read in detail. Be aware of the small print and the implications of leaving the accommodation before the rent agreement expires, conditions attaching to refund of deposits, any penalties for damage and rules about having parties.

Under-age drinking laws vary from country to country – better to find that out before you make your travel arrangements. This applies worldwide.

Other things to consider when travelling to another country/continent:

- Visas for entry and exit
- Insurance and health cover
- Extra charges with accommodation such as: water usage, refuse collection, the air conditioning costs in hot countries and heating costs in cold countries

Events and trips associated with your course require a risk assessment to be completed and approved before the event.

It is most important that you take out the necessary health and travel insurance, whether on study, work or leisure stays, and you must always get this insurance sorted *before* you leave the country, regardless of duration or geographical location. It is a small price to pay early, as in many countries where patients are unable to pay, they may not be released until the bill is paid in full.

It is so worthwhile to make an effort to speak the native language of the country you are visiting and take some time to research the culture and customs, regardless of the language of learning at your university. This is considered a compliment in most countries and the experience can be fun.

If you are travelling with friends, choose them carefully.

Looking after yourself

In this section, we will look at student well-being including aspects of physical and mental health, anxiety and stress, and self-care.

Minding your mental and physical health is essential for your personal and professional development through your years at university. Good habits take time to form. Consistency is key to changing old habits or developing new ones. It is important to identify areas for such change and development.

To develop personally and professionally we must become comfortable with *self* and we must find out more about *self*. Real growth and development come when we are comfortable with identifying areas of both strengths and weaknesses, enabling us to make choices about short- and long-term goals. In looking at self, there are many parts to consider, and in this section we break *self* into five components and explore each one and how it can impact on your life experience now and into the future.

- Physical
- Mental
- Emotional
- Spiritual
- Interpersonal communication

Reading about the various aspects of self later in this section might trigger some thoughts on how you look after yourself, how consistent you are in doing so and how you can make small changes that build over time into reaching the goal of practising good physical and mental health. First let's take a look at how we sleep and how this can affect our overall health and well-being.

In this section, there will be many exercises which you can engage in to help you establish how you can achieve better well-being. These exercises are centred around identifying gaps and strengths in the various aspects of self and in the practice of goal setting to make changes.

Sleep patterns

The quality of our sleep is a major contributor to our physical and mental health. Sleep rests the body and the brain. The recommended sleeping hours for young adults are between seven and nine hours per night. When you are sleep-deprived, poor patterns of eating and studying usually follow.

Studies show that a healthy sleep pattern reduces stress and inflammation, helps prevent and fight off disease, helps in maintaining a healthy body weight and improves concentration and memory.

There is no one solution to improving sleep patterns, however it is widely recognized that the following may be helpful in establishing consistent sleeping habits:

- Find out when you work best and try to fit in with your body rhythm. Try to limit your screen time late in the evening as this is known to negatively affect your ability to sleep.
- When you can, get out and walk in the fresh air. This can be hard to do at times but if you try to get out each day, very soon it will become a habit and you will feel fresh and energized afterwards. You will never regret taking a walk!
- Try to avoid too much caffeine and, if you can, don't drink tea or coffee late in the evening.
- It is important to look at your diet and limit your sugar intake as this gives the body false boosts. Data suggests that diets low in fibre and high in sugar negatively affect sleeping patterns.
- Avoid taking naps as they upset your natural cycle. Try to keep to a regular getting up time and going to bed time – this is difficult, particularly as a student, but try it out for a few days in succession. It will bring some regularity to your day.
- Plan on Sunday evenings how you intend to study for the week, working to realistic goals. Such planning has a settling influence on the mind as you start

the week. Try to get good study time from Monday to Wednesday, as once you reach Thursday the week is nearly over. Having achieved some progress in your studies will help you to relax and sleep will come more naturally.

Before we delve into the five aspects of self, we will look at setting goals.

Setting goals

Success is about setting and achieving goals. Goals need to be clear and practical, and have clearly defined steps which are set within a realistic time frame.

Clear Your goal is about a target you want to achieve
Realistic Is this possible for you to achieve?
Practical Do you have the necessary tools and time to achieve your goal?

For every goal achieved, always treat yourself with some form of reward. Rewards are individual to you – they can take many shapes and sizes and can be little or large. It might be a walk in the park, a bar of your favourite chocolate, a night out with friends, a long rest in the morning. The personal satisfaction achieved in the accomplishment of a defined goal may be enough reward in itself for many. Treat yourself.

Physical well-being

Do you ever stop to think about how you look after yourself, your diet and your fitness?

Feeding the body nutritionally is central to a healthy lifestyle. Keeping your body at a healthy weight can reduce risks of cancer, heart and chronic disease, improve memory and concentration skills and lead to healthy bones and a stronger immune system to fight off infection. The wave of increased obesity which is evident in our world today is leading to greater prevalence of diabetes and diabetes-related illnesses in our young people, which puts enormous pressure on our health systems and budgets. A little effort by everyone will help in the fight for a healthier world.

Eating nutritiously requires a balanced diet and developing a healthy relationship with food.

It is important to balance your diet, trying to fit in your five portions of fruit and vegetables every day, with fibre, pasta/rice/potato/cereal and some beans, pulses, meat, fish, eggs or other protein.

Some tips to develop healthy eating habits

Make a meal plan and stick to it. Don't make the plan overambitious. Start with one change each week, which could be any of the following:

- Learn how to cook a few simple meals from scratch – start with one recipe and add more as you go along

- Try to organize your shopping for the week ahead on Saturday or Sunday
- Prepare a healthy packed lunch and avoid wasting money on takeaway food or sandwiches in the campus canteen or local coffee shops
- Ensure you don't store stocks of biscuits or sweet things in your cupboard
- Drink plenty of water
- Avoid skipping meals
- Eat slowly
- Portion sizes matter – how big is your plate?
- Keep a diary of your food consumption for a few weeks and you will be surprised what you will find out about your eating habits and what you spend on satisfying them
- Try getting a few friends together to take turns in doing the cooking

Planning your eating diary for the week ahead is beneficial both to your health and well-being and to your bank balance.

If you plan your meals carefully rather than rushing to the corner shop when you are feeling hungry you are less likely to buy unhealthy foods, as at those times you are often craving a 'sugar fix'. Likewise, if you are coming home late you will be less tempted to stop at the nearest takeaway and blow half your budget in a few minutes on food that is nutritionally questionable and only satisfying in the moment.

Take a look at the 'One-pot recipes' on the BBC Good Food website.

Exercising

It is widely documented that exercise is good for us and helps the body to age well. Not only does it improve our physical well-being, but it also improves concentration and boosts mood – and helps in the fight against obesity and other diseases. Exercise does not have to mean running a marathon or swimming several lengths of an Olympic-size pool.

Simply walking is good for the mind, body and soul. While going out for a walk might not be appealing, especially in a British winter, research tells us that there are substantial benefits to a 20-minute stroll daily. Walking allows us to get in touch with nature and to meet with others in our communities. Almost everyone can get involved.

Consistency is the key to a healthy exercise regime. Setting achievable goals is crucial.

Some people find exercising easy and train for marathons and such ambitious targets. However, you may not find that exercising comes naturally to you.

If you are not exercising or find it very difficult, it is so important to start with a small goal. Try the simple things like walking instead of taking the bus, or getting off a stop or two ahead of your destination and doing the same on the way home.

Try starting with 20 minutes of exercise every day. This should be something that can be achieved quite easily as part of your daily routine,

Health, Identity and Society **91**

particularly if you have any distance to travel to campus. Getting this out of the way in the morning is good as you can face the day feeling energized and happy that you are making an effort. Try to incorporate this into your daily routine. In time you can increase this to 30 minutes and then to an hour as your fitness level and motivation increase. Listen to your body; the more you exercise, the better you will feel.

Take things at a comfortable pace, particularly if you are new to exercising. You will need to warm up and cool down properly. As you increase your exercise, you might like to try other ways such as fitness classes or swimming. Most universities have facilities for students at reduced prices to encourage better physical health, which then feeds into positive mental health.

While exercise is good for the body, supporting teams in their sporting ventures is good for the soul and a great way of joining in and meeting people.

Be sensible if taking exercise in public parks, secluded places or poorly lit areas. Your safety comes first, always.

Can you take time to answer the following questions?

- How does your physical well-being affect your study, your work, your home space?
- Do you feel positive or negative about it?
- Why?

Within the framework of the following very simple model, it might be useful to jot down what comes to mind relating to the questions above, on self and your physical well-being.

My physical well-being

Here's what I am good at	Here's what I need help with

What you can do to change

- Do you feel positive or negative about your physical well-being?
- What one change could you make to develop this part of self?
- What impact do you think any changes might have on you and on others around you?

Set your goals here to develop your physical well-being

Name the goal	Time limit	Action steps	Review	Reward	Comment

Mental well-being

Our mental health influences all that we do, how we think, feel and behave. It is an integral part of who we are and what we do from childhood to adulthood. Our mental stability manifests in how we handle stress, interact with others, react and adapt to change. Good mental health builds resilience and facilitates balanced decision-making. It allows us to be more productive and effective and to enjoy the simple pleasures of life as well as managing the more complex problems.

Can you answer the following questions?

- What are your general thoughts about 'self'?
- What is your general attitude to home life, study life and leisure time?
- What are your self-statements?
- Do you visualize yourself in positive situations?
- Do you smile much?
- Do you enjoy life?

Within the framework of the same model, it might be useful to jot down what comes to mind on the questions above and relating to self and your mental well-being.

My mental well-being

Here's what I am good at	Here's what I need help with

What you can do to change

- Do you feel positive or negative about the 'mental' part of self?
- What changes could you make to develop this part of self?
- What impact do you think any changes might have on you and your relationships with others?

Set your goals here to develop your mental well-being

Name the goal	Time limit	Action steps	Review	Reward	Comment

If you feel that you are consistently in a negative frame of mind and unable to find joy in your life, you may need to seek out the assistance of a professional who can work with you to overcome your fears and anxieties. The health service at your university will provide assistance and referrals and are there to help you find solutions. Support is also offered online, through the student services and the personal tutor service. Talking to friends and peers helps too. Often many of your concerns are also the concerns of others, and spending time over a coffee can reduce anxieties. There is no shame or embarrassment associated with seeking such assistance and all services are operated in the utmost confidentiality.

Emotional well-being

Our emotional awareness affects our physical and mental well-being. It is important to be able to express your opinions and feelings appropriately without causing stress in relationships or problems with your study. Have you ever been in the situation where you reacted quickly and deeply regretted it later on? We need to learn to be calm and think before we speak.

How we manage stress and strive for balance feeds into our emotional well-being. We need to spend time doing things we enjoy and create boundaries between our place of study, work and leisure. We need to have our home a stress-free zone. This isn't always easy, as often students are sharing with fellow students who do not respect others' values and privacy.

We all need to connect with others for our emotional well-being. It's good to get involved in societies or groups that have like-minded interests. We need to choose our friends carefully, adopting positive people into our lives. Recognize what is important to you and prioritize accordingly.

Be kind to yourself and to others. This naturally emits a positive energy, and you will find that in time you will receive kindness in abundance in return.

Can you answer these questions?

- How do you manage your feelings?
- If you feel strongly about something, how do you make that feeling known to others?
- Are you aware of other people's feelings?
- Do you allow others to express their views comfortably?
- Is your use of language appropriate to situations?

Within the framework of the same model, it might be useful to jot down what comes to mind on the questions above and relating to self and your emotional wellbeing.

My emotional well-being

Here's what I am good at	Here's what I need help with

What you can do to change

- Do you feel positive or negative about the 'emotional' aspect of self?
- What changes could you make to develop this part of self?
- What impact do you think any changes might have on you and your relationships with others?

Set your goals here to develop your emotional well-being

Name the goal	Time limit	Action steps	Review	Reward	Comment

Spiritual well-being

The spiritual aspect of self looks at the inner self, how we see our core values and the meaning and purpose of life. It's about our inner being, our reflective self and where we see ourselves belonging. For some this can be a religious experience, visiting a place of worship. More commonly today it is associated with quiet and reflective time, uninterrupted time and space for one's mind to rest and relax.

Meditation, which evolved from ancient traditions, facilitates this engagement with our spiritual self. Practising yoga, visiting nature reserves or walking in parks and near lakes or by the seaside restores the mind, body and soul and brings an air of spiritual freedom in the busy world around us.

Can you answer these questions?

- Do you feel positive or negative about the 'spiritual' aspect of self?
- Do you take time away from others and your study/work to reflect?
- Do you allow yourself a quiet time and space to reflect?
- When and how do you relax?

Within the framework of the same model, it might be useful to jot down what comes to mind relating to self and your spiritual well-being.

My spiritual well-being

Here's what I am good at	Here's what I need help with

What you can do to change

- Do you feel positive or negative about the 'spiritual' aspect of self?
- What changes could you make to develop this part of self?

- What impact do you think any changes might have on you and your relationships with others?

Set your goals here to develop your spiritual well-being

Name the goal	Time limit	Action steps	Review	Reward	Comment

All of the above exercises will take time to reflect on and complete. They are not meant to be carried out at speed. They are useful to return to intermittently as you encounter issues at various times in your university experience. You may also seek to complete them each year, consistently identifying areas for growth and development. Feedback from students who have engaged regularly with these exercises at the timing of their needs report a more focused approach to getting the most out of the university experience and preparing themselves for the world of work ahead.

Interpersonal communication

Your interpersonal communication skills are essential to succeeding at university and in your life thereafter, both from a personal and professional perspective. Being aware of how we communicate to and with others and how they respond to us shapes and forms our future relationships. These skills are an integral part of the skill set required for the modern-day workforce – skills which so far can't be replaced by artificial intelligence or machine learning.

Those with strong interpersonal skills are recognized for building healthier relationships with colleagues and their effective team working in achieving common goals. These skills are very much sought after by employers as they see good communicators as being flexible and adaptable and able to communicate across age, gender and culture.

Good interpersonal communication is also essential to building and maintaining strong personal relationships. How we interact with others in our 'home' is vital to our overall well-being, whether that is in a university residence, within a family unit or living in a shared space. Our 'home' space should feel safe and unthreatening for all who live there.

Can you answer these questions?

- How do you communicate with others?
- Do you listen or do you like to speak to have your voice heard?

- How much are you in control of what you say and do?
- How do you manage difficult situations?
- How do you interact in a team situation?
- Are you at ease socially interacting with others?
- How comfortable are you communicating with friends, family and peers?

My interpersonal communication

Here's what I am good at	Here's what I need help with

What you can do to change

- Do you feel positive or negative about the 'interpersonal communication' aspect of self?
- What changes could you make to develop this part of self?
- What impact do you think any changes might have on you and your relationships with others?

Set your goals here to develop your interpersonal communication

Name the goal	Time limit	Action steps	Review	Reward	Comment

Suicide

Unfortunately, suicide is a global phenomenon, and according to the World Health Organization is the second leading cause of death among 15- to 29-year-olds. It's a topic that nobody wants to talk about, but it is important to have the discussion and to become aware of the key signs. It is crucial to know that help is close at hand and that universities have professional staff who are well qualified to deal with students who are at risk.

Warning signs of feeling suicidal can include:

- feelings of hopelessness and helplessness
- feeling of being a burden on others
- withdrawing from social engagement and activities
- unusual and different behaviour
- extreme mood swings
- lack of interest in life
- giving away personal things

Life experiences can contribute to increased risks of suicide. These experiences can directly relate to the loss of friends or family, relationship break-ups, terminal illnesses of friends or family, depression, poor health, drug or alcohol use.

If you experience any of these feelings of desperation and loss of hope, or know somebody else who may be at risk, seek help from the university counselling services which are confidential, and set up solely for the well-being of the students attending. Regular workshops are run to assist students in building up good mental health where the focus is targeted on the positive aspects of life and dealing with one day at a time. Students who may not wish to use the student services at university should also be aware that external professional services such as the Samaritans are available to all who are in need of help.

See 'Student Health' under the Useful Links and Resources section at the back of this book for further information on other services available.

Anxiety

The feeling of anxiety is a normal and common human response and experience. It is the level at which we experience it which determines how it can interfere with the way we live our lives. Anxiety affects how we think and behave and is demonstrated by feelings of panic, leaving us in situations where we can't think straight and make sound decisions.

Anxiety can be feelings of fear or worry and can range from the mild to the severe. It is not unusual for our younger population to experience anxiety attacks, and recent research is telling us that this is now a growing problem in younger children in primary education.

Feelings of unease that spiral out of control leave the person helpless and the normal things in life can become insurmountable problems: fear of examinations, fear of failure, fear of what's going to happen, fear of losing loved ones, fear of interviews.

Anxiety is a common condition but one which can have a detrimental effect on your daily life. If you feel that you are very stressed and suffering from anxiety, talk to a friend, a fellow student or your tutor. Please seek out help from the many student services available to you at your university.

Substance use and abuse

There is always concern relating to alcohol consumption and drug intake in the university student population and every year brings its own tragic stories. Every effort is made by universities to keep students safe and well advised regarding the side effects of all drug consumption.

Given the intoxicating effects of excessive alcohol intake and the resulting often most unacceptable behaviours, it is wise to adopt the policy of eating before drinking. If you form this habit at a younger age, then this practice will remain with you for life. Unfortunately, some students find themselves at the centre of negative encounters with the law. Such encounters are almost always associated with excessive alcohol intake.

It is important to point out that it is against the law to sell drink to those under 18 years.

When you are over 18, you must also understand that you are no longer a minor, and if charges are brought against you and you appear before a judge in court, you will be treated like an adult – a family account of your good behaviour will hold little value. Should this happen to you, your criminal record may be about to begin. A criminal record will determine your freedom to work and travel overseas, and in many cases it can preclude you from holding positions in government office or the teaching and caring professions, to mention just a few.

The consumption of illegal drugs is an unlawful offence in England and carries severe penalties. Students need to educate themselves about the side effects of illegal drugs, physical and mental, both short term and long term.

There is also growing concern regarding the misuse of prescribed drugs and over-the-counter medications. Students need to become better informed about the effects of all these drugs. Advice is available through the university health/counselling services.

Developing resilience

Resilience can be defined as an ability to react to difficulties that challenge us in life – our ability to bounce back in the face of adversity.

Developing resilience is an incremental process where we take control of how we respond to the challenges that we are faced with over time and life. Things happen in life that we have no control over and yet our ability to respond

Health, Identity and Society **101**

to these life events determines how we mould and shape our future reactions to similar or more challenging life events.

Resilience demands strong problem-solving skills and the ability to set goals and action steps to overcome these challenging events. We can develop resilience through the formation of strong networks, and the adoption of positive people – the 'can do' people – into our circles. We also need to bring some humility into our lives and to practise gratitude. Keeping a journal of the various challenges we meet and how we respond is useful for this purpose. It is what we learn from these challenges and how we can develop our ability to cope with similar challenges ahead that develops our resilience.

Seeking help

We have looked at the many support services which are made available to you during your time at university and explored them in a variety of ways in this section and in other parts of the book.

The continued reference to these services reflects the importance of how and why we should seek help and stand proud that we are trying to take control of problems before they escalate to a level that will drive absences from your university duties.

Seeking help is often not seen as the most obvious solution by those who are going through challenging times. What is important is to recognize when you need to get help. This is often noticed first by your peers, friends, family, tutors or others in your circle.

If you notice that a friend or classmate is showing consistent signs of mood change, and may be in some financial or emotional difficulty, then a quiet word of encouragement may be all that is needed. We saw the perfect example of this in the recent series of *Normal People* when the lead male actor Connell, a university student, went to a counsellor at university to seek help in dealing with his friend's suicide.

If you notice that your mood is down for a number of weeks and that the light is hard to find in life, then maybe you might need to have a chat with a professional in one of the confidential services that are offered at your university. Likewise, if you notice a similar situation developing with one of your peers, you may be in a position to encourage them to make use of the relevant services.

Troubleshooting section

Top tips
- Get to know yourself better and try to seek help when you need it
- Try to look out for others who may need help
- Seek out help which is available to you and your fellow students through your tutors and the support services at your university

This could be you

My course expects us to work in teams, but I find it difficult

Working with others is an essential skill to develop as an undergraduate, and it requires good interpersonal skills. You need to be confident in your own views and contributions, but also to listen to others. You should always make your point in a polite way, and sometimes the consensus will not be to go with your view. If group working gets really difficult, talk to a member of staff or your tutor. There may be workshops at the university to help you manage team relationships more effectively.

I feel anxious and have stopped going to my lectures

Do you know why you are feeling anxious? Could it be that you are struggling to keep up academically? Do you feel you are fitting in socially with your peer group? Are you worried about finances? Do you feel lonely or homesick? Have others stopped going to lectures too?

Try to find a friend or fellow student to chat things over. There may be a common problem that you are unaware of and working together might present some solutions. It's so good to talk to others if you can. You might find it easier to talk to your tutor or to someone attached to the many student advisory services on offer to you. Perhaps you might be more comfortable using a telephone or online service? Letting the situation continue will only serve to make matters worse and you will fall behind very quickly in your studies. Tutors and those in the advisory services are very experienced in dealing with these situations and will help get you back on track.

International students

I am falling behind with my work and I can't sleep

When you are studying in a foreign language the work can take longer to complete. Plan your time carefully, and review whether you are allowing sufficient time for each task you need to complete. If you do this and still run out of time, keep a diary to discover which tasks are taking longer than you anticipated. Then consider if there are any university services that could help you develop your skills in these areas. Sleep rests the body and the brain. See page 88 for tips on how to develop a good sleeping pattern.

Building employability skills

Build your personal skills and confidence by completing the exercises outlined in this section. This will stand you in good stead when preparing for interviews for internships or jobs in the future.

Part V

Looking Ahead

In your second year the university will continue to engage with you in delivering the best possible student experience, but you in turn must also continue to engage in order to make the most of the experience and enjoy the variety of opportunities and services on offer. At this stage of your university education, your university is embedding best practice to develop students to meet the rapidly changing world challenges that they will face as graduates into the future. Graduates of the future will need to be mobile, employable and active citizens contributing to the community, but above all they will need to be resilient.

In Section 1 we will look at what lies ahead, dealing particularly with settling into your second year. This includes building on all aspects of your personal and professional development and looks at many of the areas you can explore while planning for your future after graduation.

In Section 2 we will look at the third/fourth/final year of your university experience and how you can best prepare yourself for the world of work. This section will help you to make informed choices and you can pick and choose what is most relevant to meet your particular needs.

Section 1: Preparing for your second year

When you successfully transition to your second year at university, there are an equal number of opportunities and pitfalls that are useful to know about as you begin the year. These can be categorized as follows:

- Academic
- Social
- Making more friends
- Part-time jobs
- Internships
- Volunteering
- Work placements
- Preparing for graduate employment

Academic

The second year of study can be somewhat of an anticlimax. Student retention continues to be an issue and while not at all as prevalent as in the first year, it is not uncommon for students to drop out in this second year.

You might feel that the major focus seems to be on the first and final year students around you and often the enthusiastic nature of the application to first-year university life may wane in this year. There is less obvious support immediately available, or so it can seem, and the work often counts towards your final degree, so the pressure can seem more intense.

The university continues to offer support services to students, but many universities report a reluctance by students to take up these services at this critical time in their grasp of new academic material.

It is important to try to get to know your lecturers, their assistants and your tutor and build on these relationships. Try to become a more active participant at seminars/tutorials and any other interactions appropriate to such participation. Take note of how you are assessed over the course of the semester and academic year. Assessment models may be quite different to your first year and you don't want to find any nasty surprises that are too late to fix.

In relation to assessment it is worth understanding more about how your degree will be awarded. This may be detailed in the handbook or university regulations, and the Students' Union or your personal tutor may be useful sources of information. Like your first year, the handbook is key to unlocking these surprises early on. Read your handbook carefully and read it often as you progress through your many and varied assignments during the academic year.

There is undoubtedly an increased academic workload in the second year at university, and students who perform well in the first year can often underperform in their second year. Your priorities change as you grow into university life in your second year, and often students find that the academic challenges are more difficult as more complex theories and models are introduced. To guard against this, prepare well for your lectures by reading material and undertaking preparatory activities in advance. This will make your life much easier and the lectures more interesting. It is also very useful to rewrite notes within the same day of your lectures as this will aid memory and retention.

One of the bigger risks with second-year students is that complacency can set in. Don't let this be you. Keep a firm control on your journey and attend all lectures, seminars, tutorials, labs etc., seeking out help from your tutor and the university services along the way. It is important to recognize when you need help and to seek out assistance from the many academic services available to enable you to make the most of your studies and your university experience.

Social

Your first-year accommodation is either allocated to you or you choose it based on factors such as cost, location and facilities. In the second year you are able to choose who you live with. Many students opt to, or are required to, move out of campus accommodation or halls of residence, as more often priority is given to first years and international students.

Students generally like to live in a private sector shared house, offering a more independent and often cheaper lifestyle. Groups of students agree to live together, and then view properties to rent as a group. Typically, you have your own room, and share the kitchen, bathroom and lounge. The groups are often formed around Christmas in the first year, as viewings and lettings take place and are agreed early in the new year, while you are still in your first year.

If you miss out on this you may have to take a room in a house with people you don't know, which can present challenges. There is, however, a risk that you fall out with the group of people you decided to live with between Christmas and the start of the new academic year, so choose carefully. You don't have to live with your best friends – indeed visiting other houses is part of the fun. But make sure you are not living with people that will be difficult to get on with – e.g. not willing to keep the communal areas clean and tidy, especially if this is important to you, or having parties/friends round late at night if you are an early riser.

In second year, you are making choices about what to do and what not to do based on your first-year experience. You are now part of the university community and are somewhat used to breaking into new social situations, living on a low budget and sharing accommodation. You are no longer daunted by the content of your handbook and the many often conflicting work and study expectations.

Your social life is vital for growth and development. This year you can be more selective about your pursuits. If you spent a lot of your first-year partying and losing focus on your studies, now might be the time for a reality check and to refocus. Likewise, if you did not engage in social interaction in the first year, you might want to introduce some interaction by joining a society or club where there is a mutual interest.

There will be something to suit all tastes at your university. It's always good to take up something new each year, try different things, spread your horizons, meet new people and live new experiences.

Making more friends

This year is time to work on building your relationships with your friends. The memories will follow and be treasured. As a second-year student you will meet new people and make new friends if you choose to. These friendships can be academically or socially led. Over the course of your studies, you will gravitate towards more like-minded students as you share common interests through the specialized subjects you pick and the tutorial experiences that this brings. Where there is a strong coincidence of interest, students are known to gather for extended breakfasts to debate the many theories and opinions articulated at the early morning lectures. The same applies to the online transmission of lectures where students break out into virtual groups.

Interest in societies is extended in the second year as you become more confident in choosing different ways of spending your recreational time. Clubs and societies that you might have dismissed in your first year may look more appealing to you in this second year as you have had time to stand back and reflect on things you engaged in, or didn't, before. These clubs and societies have strong online presence so there is added advantage if you can't attend campus for personal or societal reasons, such as the Covid-19 pandemic which has challenged both the learning delivery and social experience of university life.

Making friends takes time and effort. Get involved and grow and build your network. By making that extra effort now you will reap rewards in the years ahead.

Part-time jobs

Balancing part-time work and study can be tricky as the academic demands on your course of study increase. The need to earn money to fund the educational experience remains a priority for many throughout the calendar year. It is important to have a monthly budget and to plan in advance how that budget can be funded. Money worries are stressful.

We can see work patterns evolving in our society and how economic factors influence these patterns over the years. Supply and demand dictates opportunity, and has been the case over generations.

If you have a part-time job that fits in well with your academic timetable and doesn't interfere with your academic performance or progress, then you are one of the luckier students.

There are many schools of thought in the learning community regarding part-time work during the university years. The conflict of earning vs learning arises. There are distinct advantages to this type of work as it is financially and professionally rewarding. It also builds networks, strengthens your CV and develops skills which will be attractive to employers in the long run. The decision about part-time work is largely down to the individual and how he or she can balance the academic workload, deadlines and study commitments. Many can balance the two with ease, however this requires a lot of focus and discipline and above all, good time management.

Students who have very demanding academic schedules and a lot of laboratory work or clinical placements usually prefer to apply themselves solely to their studies during the academic year to achieve top results, and focus on earning money during the summer months. This could take the form of paid internships, which will be addressed in a later section.

Some universities strongly recommend against working part-time while on particular courses. Others are more relaxed in their approach. Some will say that you are at university to study and in employment to work and not to confuse the two!

There is certainly an expectation that you are a full-time student, even if your contact time is not all day every day. Work needs to be in addition to your course contact time and independent learning, not instead of it. On the other hand, there is growing recognition and acceptance that students also need to work. Sometimes the timetable is blocked to allow some weekdays that you can use for working rather than studying, but then you need to undertake the additional studying in the evenings or at the weekend.

It is probably wise to take your lead from those who run your course of study and from students in the year ahead of you as they will be in a good position to guide you in making the right decision for you. However, at the end of the day, only you can make that judgement call to suit your situation.

Internships

Internships vary between universities. Many, but not all courses provide this opportunity to students. This is a very competitive process and attention to detail in your application is important.

The emphasis is on students finding and applying for internships directly to companies offering them. The careers service can point you in the direction of the information about internships available that are relevant to your discipline or interests, but can also help you more, through individual interviews and group workshops. It is really worth taking advantage of these opportunities.

Internships take place at the end of your penultimate year, and ideally can result in securing graduate employment, which means that in your final year you can devote your time to your studying. This does not, however, happen for the majority of students. In order to secure an internship, especially with a major graduate employer in a competitive sector, you need to start networking with employers by attending events and undertaking other opportunities for work experience. These, together with an expected graduation with a II.1 or higher, are often required to secure a summer internship.

The purpose of the internship is to further develop your understanding of how your discipline of study is applied to solving practical problems in the workplace, dealing with real-life issues.

Internships usually take place during the summer months and can range from 4 to 12 weeks' duration. You will discover the link between theory and practice and how your knowledge can be applied to the challenges you will meet day to day in the workplace.

Applications for internships generally open early in the first semester but can run throughout the academic year. You need to be proactive in your search for a placement and to check regularly for updates from the administrative office dealing with internships at your university.

Internships give students an added advantage when seeking employment as graduates in their field. Many students who are taken on for these internships mid university are offered a placement on graduation. In some cases, students may be offered a research internship, which can be facilitated at your own university or within a network of universities across the world, depending on visa restrictions. It is important to conduct yourself in a professional manner at all times. This also relates to timekeeping and dress code.

Similarly, the employer gets to see you in action and establishes if you are a good fit in the workforce, if you are professional, reliable, flexible and adaptable. They need to be convinced by your actions that they should hire you.

Not all universities will offer assistance in setting up internships. In most cases you will have to do the groundwork. Check this out early on at your university.

Volunteering

Volunteering provides an alternative way of gaining relevant work experience, and in some sectors may be a more viable option as there are few or no internships.

Many organizations seek to meet their strategic goals in relation to corporate and social responsibility by creating volunteering opportunities.

Volunteering is a noble activity whether you are working at your local charity shop or working abroad. Volunteering has no time limits – it can be for days, weeks, months or longer.

Fundraising for local charities by running events is good for the soul and simultaneously facilitates the development of new skills. Online events are becoming increasingly popular as the world continues to embrace the digital age.

There is little doubt that volunteering boosts confidence and provides a platform for meeting new friends and building networks while adding value to your CV. It is well noted that alumni gather frequently to support charities which they fostered while volunteering during their student days at university.

If you are planning to go abroad for volunteering work, you will need to do your research and prepare and plan well to make the most of the opportunity. Working abroad as a volunteer can be challenging and not for the faint-hearted. There are usually significant costs associated with this, which will include travel, accommodation and living expenses.

Volunteering is a personally satisfying endeavour and makes a positive difference to society, giving you the opportunity to acquire lifelong transferable skills.

Visit the student services at your university, who may be able to assist you in finding these opportunities.

Volunteering is coordinated by universities, who ensure that the opportunities are safe and suitable. This can be done by student services or the careers service, and the Students' Union. Many of the opportunities involve volunteering two or three hours per week and fit alongside studying; there are also opportunities to undertake a more intensive activity, e.g. for a week. This could include redecorating a community centre, tidying up a local park or helping with disadvantaged children's holidays, to name but a few. Many volunteering roles involve working with children and vulnerable people, and you have to be DBS (Disclosure and Barring Service) checked. This can take some time and may have cost implications. Late submission of documentation may mean you will miss out on your volunteering experience, so it's best to start your preparations in good time.

Work placements

Many courses have work placements as an optional or compulsory component, and these can be local, elsewhere in the UK, or overseas. If the work placement is integrated into the course, students must complete this placement in accordance with the terms set out by the university. These placements can be full-time, e.g. for a number of weeks, or part-time (so many hours per week), and they can range from clinical to professional settings. Generally the university collaborates closely with the relevant sector/industry in setting them up, monitoring development and progress and seeking regular feedback over the time of the placement. When placements are compulsory there may be little room for choice, although this may vary between institutions and disciplines. The university will usually ensure that each student experiences a range of placement opportunities across the course.

If you have particular concerns (perhaps related to fulfilling other responsibilities), speak to your tutor as early as possible, but recognize that you signed up to the placements as part of the course.

You may be entitled to financial support for travel or accommodation while you are on placement, but it may well be that you are expected to pay the costs. If you experience financial hardship you should approach student services as most English universities have emergency support funds that can offer loans or bursaries. There may also be additional bursary support available to help with buying clothes or uniform, travel or accommodation costs.

Where placements are optional you are likely to have more choice about the type of placement, its location, its duration and whether it is full- or part-time. Your tutor, course leader or careers office can help you to identify a suitable opportunity, but it may be up to you to make the first contact and arrange the details. Work placements provide an excellent opportunity to put into practice what you have learned, or to develop connections between theory and practice, to develop graduate skills and to make contacts that may help you to secure graduate employment. There are additional costs involved, so think carefully about what these additional costs will be and how you can meet them – and do approach the university to find out about financial support that is available to you. Some universities also offer mentoring support to help throughout your placement experience.

In some courses (such as language programmes) overseas placements may be required, but you may also choose to work in a placement overseas. This will create some further challenges, but many new opportunities. A key factor will be to plan this early, and to make a start on developing any required foreign language skills (which will depend on the nature of your placement).

Think carefully about the type of work placement that is likely to maximize the benefits to you – you might get offered a graduate employment opportunity. Research demonstrates much better employment outcomes for students who have undertaken work placements. It is your occasion to shine. In all work placements, a professional work ethic is expected at all times. This exposure will provide you with the opportunity to understand the relationship between your academic study and the world of work, to gain transferable skills, both a character and work reference and the prospect of a job offer on graduation.

Preparing for graduate employment

It is so important to take an interest at an early stage in what's going on at your university such as job fairs, seminars and public talks. Develop a sense of enquiry into what is happening around you regarding opportunities in the workforce not only within your year but in the years ahead. Observe where there is action and follow it – you might be surprised where it can lead. Start working on your CV and see what gaps you can identify, and think about ways that you can develop existing and new skills to fill these gaps. Careers services offer workshops on developing your CV.

Think about how you might gain work experience or if there are any internships available which can run over the summer months. Get in early to have a choice as these vacancies fill up quickly and can be oversubscribed. Your second year is a time to reflect on why you are at university, what you are hoping to achieve and how this can lead you towards a career path. Over the remainder of your time at university, your aspirations may change. However, any groundwork done early will prove fruitful in the long run.

Your second year brings a need for more adjustment to the academic and social demands of university life. It also presents new challenges on the social, financial and domestic fronts. You may be living with new people, struggling with balancing your finances and concerned about your social engagement with others.

Pick your friends carefully, and who you live with even more carefully. Those you live with influence how you eat, sleep, study, socialize and network. Your home should be a safe, secure and stress-free place.

Over this year your sense of purpose and identity will be further challenged and yet become clearer. You will begin to identify gaps in your personal and professional development which can be addressed strategically, in a positive and deliberate manner over the course of your remaining time at university.

Section 2: Third year/fourth year and beyond

You are now either two-thirds or halfway towards earning your degree and entering the final stages, be that on a three- or four-year course. You have done well to reach this point and as you look around you and see some vacant places, you may become more encouraged to put in your strongest effort to make the most of the remainder of your university experience. Your third year is an important year and critical decisions will be called upon to direct the focus of your studies and deliberate more about what direction you might like to take after graduation.

At this stage, you need to think about jobs that might feed into your degree and how you can use university resources to help you achieve your goals. It is also a time to look into postgraduate studies and whether this type of study can bring added value to your degree and expand your skill set in preparation for the world of work. The final year(s) of your time at university will fly by so any early research will be most beneficial as you try to achieve high academic grades and simultaneously look for opportunities.

Whether you opt to engage in postgraduate study or to enter the world of work after graduation, both searches require considerable time and effort to get the right fit.

There are many avenues for you to explore prior to the completion of your university degree. It would be useful to focus on the areas most relevant to your skill set and your needs at your specific stage of learning. These areas can range from a gap year to internships, from CV and interview preparation to looking for work, from understanding more about intrapreneurship and entrepreneurship, coping with the changing future of work and how the university degree fits with your journey of lifelong learning.

Different areas are presented in an order open to you to pick and choose. This section will assist you in making decisions about what might be useful to navigate in the final stages of your university journey.

We will look at the following areas:

- University resources
- Job fairs
- Internships
- Graduate schemes
- Gap year
- Looking for work
    - Researching the organization
    - CV preparation
    - Completing the application form
    - The covering letter
    - The interview
    - Coping with rejection
- The future of work
- Employability
- Entrepreneurial spirit
- Intrapreneurial spirit
- The value of a university education
- Postgraduate study
- Lifelong learning
- The gig economy
- Global connectivity

University resources

Your university has leads into just about all avenues in the wider world of business and the economy, both private and public sector and in the voluntary sector, non-governmental organizations and non-profit organizations. University offices spend a lot of time building relationships with the local, national and international community of employers, and through these networks facilitate occasion for these employers to access the most suitable talent pool to fit their needs.

Careers advice is readily available to all students and hopefully you will have started that journey with them at this stage of your studies. If not, arrange an appointment as soon as possible and seek to attend the many workshops that are provided for you. Access to an online portal relating to jobs is part of this support. Advice on CV compilation, letters of introduction, completion of application forms and tips relating to the interview are all part of this service. Seek these services out early in the year and book your slot. It will get very busy as the academic year gets up and running.

These services remain available for some time after graduation, when the university continues to offer support to past students in helping them to navigate their job searches.

Job fairs

There are many approaches taken by universities to job fairs and recruitment events. These can take place on campus, at an independent venue, in another city or country or online. In 2020/21 we saw a direct shift in the way these fairs were conducted due to the coronavirus pandemic. This presented a new set of problems as the world of work began to change more towards a digital focus throughout the university's design and delivery of learning and support. Attending online interviews will also be covered later in this section.

Job fairs are for everybody at the university to explore, whether they are looking at what is currently available or what might become available in the near future. This is a wonderful opportunity to have an informal discussion with representatives from particular organizations and to see and hear how things are on the ground.

Employers attending job fairs that are held on campus, online or offline, have the added advantage of having built up a relationship with the university and will have a reason to look for graduates from particular courses. They will also expect that future graduates will be of a similar calibre. A word of warning: always assume you are being interviewed when you engage with any member of a recruitment team, young or old, in person at fairs online or offline, or by phone on any subject matter.

Whatever avenue you pursue regarding these fairs, you will need to have your updated CV to hand for distribution. Be sure to follow up communication with a copy of your CV by email, which demonstrates your interest in a particular role or in potential roles that may emerge over time. It also creates a paper trail and consequently easier access to you.

Your tutor may also be a source of assistance in helping you carve out a career path and identifying any notable improvement in skills that you might benefit from. Check out the many workshops available to you at your university.

Internships

Internships have been covered earlier, in Section 1; however, it is important to point out that internships can continue in the summer following your final year examinations. The same rules apply to any internship.

Internships are opportunities for the employer to establish if you can do the required work and that you have a willingness and ability to be trained further if necessary. Above all, the internship process will establish that you are responsible, reliable and adaptable and fit into the culture of the organization. You too must feel that you are a good fit for the work.

Graduate schemes

These are structured training programmes which take in graduates from various disciplines with a particular set of skills. Graduates are taken in at entry level and exposed to the various functions and areas of the organization. These are paid positions and are considered a favourable option to develop your career.

Graduate schemes are highly competitive with strict criteria for entry, and are not as plentiful as graduate jobs. The careers advisory service at your university will be able to give you more information. It would be advantageous to seek out a graduate who is (or has been) on one of the schemes who might be able to assist you with your application and how you might approach the interview.

It is typical to undergo psychometric tests and participate in assessments as part of the screening process for these graduate schemes. Applications usually open early in the academic year and there are set cut-off points for submission.

Increasingly employers are using graduate assessment centres to conduct tests to help select suitable candidates. These assessments can be daunting for students. Typical questions can relate to verbal and numerical reasoning, personality and motivation, situational judgement etc. Reach out to the careers advisory service at your university who will direct you to appropriate resources to prepare adequately for this type of assessment. The Students' Union office may also be in a position to assist.

Salaries on graduate schemes can be quite attractive but these positions do not come with a guarantee of a job afterwards. However, the experience looks good on your CV and is received well by potential employers.

Gap year

Taking a 'gap year' was originally defined as a year taken by students wanting a break from studies in between school and university. However, now the term has broadened to include a break in studies for an academic year at any stage, often taken after graduation. Most students look for paid work during this time, however many take up a volunteering role, which is addressed in Section 1.

It is important to understand why you might wish to take a gap year and also to be mindful of the advantages and disadvantages of making such a decision.

Advantages

- It gives you time to travel and experience new cultures and languages
- It gives you the opportunity to follow your dreams and interests
- It can be great fun
- It can provide a good opportunity to save money to fund your studies
- It can impress employers
- You can learn a new set of transferable skills, which looks good on your CV
- It affords time to reflect on your study, career path and values in life

Disadvantages

- It can be expensive
- You can lose the study momentum
- It might be a lonely experience
- You will have to join a different year group if you plan to return to university

Employers have mixed views about gap years. Generally, they will look favourably on this time out as a well-planned and executed year away demonstrates adaptability, flexibility and an ability to deal with the unexpected. It is important to remember that planning a gap year takes a lot of time and may distract you from the academic demands of your course. Preparation is key to its success.

Looking for work

Graduate positions generally become available after graduation, but the application process often starts some months earlier, depending on the position and the employer. You may be fortunate enough to have been offered a position following an internship or work placement earlier in your studies. Graduate positions tend to have a quicker turnaround time than internships or graduate schemes. Unlike graduate schemes, graduate positions can be found in small or large firms, start-ups or long-established businesses. The variety is endless.

There are many places to look for work. Job searching is a task that requires serious time, commitment and attention to detail. A good starting point is with the careers office at your university. Advisors there are familiar with where graduates from your course have found work placed and the alternative paths they may have chosen following graduation. They have links with employers, government, agencies and entrepreneurs both at home and abroad. It is important to build a positive relationship with the advisor appointed to your discipline.

Job fairs, as referred to on page 112, are organized regularly by your university to facilitate engagement between the student body and employers. This proves very fruitful for all concerned and many students are hired on the basis of this interaction.

Your network is a vital tool in your job search. List all the people you know and how you know them, and where they and their families/friends work and live. Consider which of them you might talk to about any future ideas or plans. Try to find a role model in the industry you are targeting and find out how he or she started the career journey. Many organizations work on referrals from their existing workforce.

Graduates in employment are always willing to talk to others and share some tips and advice they may have received along the way. This particularly applies when moving to different countries and across different cultures.

A strong social media presence, for the right reasons, is important in your job search. Take a good look at your profile on all platforms you use and put yourself in a potential employer's place. How do you look and sound? What image do you portray? While news of nights out might be interesting to fellow students, it presents nothing but negative images to potential employers. If you put the information in the public eye – it will come back to bite you! Posts stored on any platform are almost impossible to remove.

You may be afforded opportunities to engage with the alumni of your university, who are more than helpful in offering advice and guidance to new graduates entering the world of work. The value of the alumni body at any university is endless and over time you will be invited to network at various organized university events. Engaging on an ongoing basis benefits all concerned.

Don't forget to actively follow up any employment leads you make and to do so quickly as minds don't retain information easily in this rapidly moving digital age. In spite of the many troubles in our world, people like to be asked to assist and are delighted when there is follow-up. Sending a 'thank you' note means a lot and keeps doors open for those who follow in the same path as you.

Researching the organization

It is essential to research the organization thoroughly before you prepare the final draft of your CV or complete an application form. Not only will you be able to glean a lot of information about how the organization functions and the services it offers, but this research will also give you an understanding of how you might fit in with its ethos and culture.

Your knowledge of the organization will send a strong message to a prospective employer that you are interested in working for the company. You may also get insight into their hiring processes and who might be interviewing you for the role. Find out whether your values are compatible with theirs. You can demonstrate this knowledge at the interview and ask relevant questions.

Knowing a lot about the organization will not only improve your self-confidence in preparing for interview but it will also reassure your potential employer that you are a serious candidate and a potentially good fit for the position advertised.

CV preparation

Employers want to appoint the best people.

Your CV is centred around your story, about how your skills, knowledge and experience make you the best candidate. It takes a considerable amount of time to prepare a good CV, which should be no longer than two pages. CVs are important when you are cold-calling or working with recruitment agencies. Applications forms will be dealt with later in this section.

Your CV needs to be tailored to the criteria specified in the job advertisement. If you are sending a CV, you will generally be asked for a covering letter (see later in this section for more on writing the covering letter).

Your CV is your first marketing tool. You are the second one – would you hire you? How can you match the job profile? If you think you can, how do you propose to relate this to your future employer at interview?

You must prepare a different CV for every job and a different covering letter to send with it. Don't make the mistake of sending the updated CV to the wrong person. Ensure that all communication is free from spelling errors, slang words or colloquialisms, and that it is laid out clearly and without clutter. Do not rely on spellcheck as it will not pick up where you have used the wrong word, as can be seen in the examples in Table 3. Make every word count.

If you are contacted by email take time in responding, ensuring that equal attention is given to how you respond, which will make an impression. All applications must be tailored to the job on offer and the specific competencies required.

Completing the application form

Completing your CV is time well spent in preparation for completing application forms.

Application forms are used widely and are usually submitted without a CV or covering letter. It is important to answer every question asked, giving

Table 3 Examples of spellcheck errors

principle or principal	personal or personnel
accept or except	all right or alright
advice or advise	sight or site
affect or effect	right or write or rite
eminent or imminent	your or you're
farther or further	there or their or they're
for or four	

Table 4 Action words

Achieved	Doubled	Persuaded
Assisted	Established	Planned
Collaborated	Evaluated	Presented
Completed	Generated	Reorganized
Conducted	Improved	Secured
Coordinated	Increased	Set up
Created	Influenced	Simplified
Defined	Innovated	Streamlined
Delivered	Introduced	Supervised
Designed	Managed	Wrote
Developed	Negotiated	
Devised	Organized	

relevant information and strictly adhering to word counts and the required layout.

On some occasions you may be asked for both a CV and application form. If this is the case, be sure that they tie in well together. You will need a bank of action words like those in Table 4 to assist you in describing your achievements to date regardless of the type of application submitted.

The covering letter

The covering letter serves as an introduction to the employer demonstrating succinctly why you have applied for the position and how you see yourself as a suitable candidate for the role. Try to keep it short and relevant and no more than three paragraphs long.

In the first paragraph, you introduce yourself, the reason you are writing and how you heard about the position. In the second paragraph, writing clearly and concisely, state your qualifications, giving examples of relevant skills for the role.

In the third paragraph you conclude politely and reiterate your interest and request to meet for interview.

Use keywords from the job description and the advertisement. The language you use throughout your application should be tailored to the specific job role advertised.

The interview

If you are called for a formal job interview this means that you are in with a serious chance of getting the job. This is your time to tell your story and to shine.

Job interviews are very stressful. They are stressful for the applicants, but remember they are also stressful for the interviewers who are under enormous pressure to pick the right person for the job. This is one of the reasons why employers like to attend job fairs at universities to engage with students as often and as early as possible.

Check out your social media sites to see how you are portrayed and what a prospective employer might think about your profile.

The interview, like any presentation, can be viewed in terms of three parts: the opening, the body and the conclusion.

The opening gives a first and lasting impression. Please arrive on time and be aware of cultural differences, how you look and how you greet. Dress appropriately for the interview. Dress for where you want to be, not where you are. If in doubt, dress more conservatively. First impressions count.

The same applies to interviews conducted online. When engaging in a virtual interview, you treat it with the same attention and respect as if it were a face-to-face interview. Ensure that your space is private, free from noise and interruptions, and that you are dressed appropriately, using a simple backdrop with a clutter-free space in the background. Mute your sound until you are ready to be admitted to the interview room.

The first question might be something along the lines of: 'Tell us a bit about yourself' or 'Take us through your CV' or 'Why did you apply for the job?' or 'Any trouble getting here?', or it might be a polite exchange/questioning about something which is current in the news. Every question that you are asked gives you an opportunity to respond in your favour, demonstrating your communication style and your ability to relate your answer to the role you have applied for.

The body of the interview is the time when you get down to the business of demonstrating how you, your skills, experience and motivation for the position will make you the preferred candidate. Everything you have written in your covering letter, CV or application form may be raised so it is important to know your own application. Even if you think a question won't be asked, you must be prepared that it will. The questioning style may be one of open-ended questions or it may be competency-based. This helps the employer to establish if you have the skills required.

Questions using the competency-based model usually start with 'Tell us about a time when …' or 'Describe a situation when …'. During this style of interview, you will be expected to respond by highlighting a situation, relating what actions you took and what the outcome was. You would also need to be able to explain what lessons you learned from the situation, and whether and why you might do things differently if you were placed in the same situation again.

You should always be clear and concise in your answers, giving sufficient detail with examples. Leave time for other questions and your chance to shine. Look for non-verbal cues. If you are unsure of what you have been asked, ask for the question to be repeated or rephrased.

Interviewees become increasingly nervous when they hear 'Have you any questions for us?' Avoid asking questions about annual leave and sick leave entitlements. You might like to know when you might hear if you have been successful or you may be interested in any professional development opportunities. At the end of the interview, it is polite to thank the panel and a perfect opportunity to refresh their memory by reminding them in a few short sentences as to exactly how you are the ideal candidate for the job.

The closing is the final impression, so you need to make it memorable in the most positive way. It is a time when you can ask questions, but most importantly it is an opportunity to work on your own sales pitch, how you see yourself as being the ideal candidate and leaving your potential employer feeling that:

- You want the job
- You have the necessary skills to do the job or can easily adapt to acquire them
- You will do the job
- You will fit into the team and the culture of the organization

If there are gaps on your CV, you will be asked about them. Can you account for them? If not, why not?

Try not to worry if you are nervous. This is normal and nerves can be converted to positive energy. Be truthful, be enthusiastic and be the solution to the employer's problem.

The interview finishes when you have left the interview and are out of sight of the building or the laptop is switched off.

The careers advisory service at your university will have support in place to assist you in CV preparation and interview techniques. It is important that you avail of these services when they are offered.

Coping with rejection

The process of job hunting is a difficult journey for many and is highly competitive today. You may find yourself in the position of receiving a rejection letter or perhaps even more than one. The availability of jobs at any time is market dependent and when demand exceeds supply, such as in recession times, the need to think outside the box becomes greater.

Try not to get too disheartened when you fail to get called for interview. When you receive a rejection letter, try to establish why you were not called for interview and work positively towards learning from the experience. This could relate to a poorly completed application form or a lack of focus in sending in a tailored and complete application, or it might be an obvious gap in experience, skills or qualifications.

If you have been called for interview but have been unsuccessful in getting the job, constructive feedback may be made available to you establishing why you didn't make that final hurdle. This could relate to the strong talent pool of other final candidates or it could relate to a poor presentation of yourself or perhaps a weak interview style. In this situation feedback will assist you in identifying the gaps. You should take comfort from the fact that you were shortlisted for interview. A higher level of preparation and practice for further interviews will make you a better candidate for another role.

Career experts can assist in identifying the gaps in your application and help you to prepare tailored solutions for specific job roles, together with running mock interviews with you. The mock interview is hugely beneficial to every candidate. Every job role will look for different competencies at different levels. It is vital that your complete application and performance at interview relates to these competencies and reflects your ability and willingness to work at the level sought.

The future of work

The future of work is here. The advent and growth of the digital age together with climate change and the threat of world disasters and pandemics greatly influences where and how we work today. There is no certainty ahead and many of the jobs over the coming decades have yet to be defined. Job searching is not an easy task, as we have written about in the last section. It is particularly difficult in depressed economies where many are being made redundant.

We know the days of a career for life and the golden handshake with a pension pot are well gone. Most graduates today will experience a few different careers and many jobs in their working lives. Many will become self-employed.

The importance of upskilling and lifelong learning cannot be overemphasized as existing skills become redundant and the world of work demands constant change. Learning how to learn at university equips the graduate with a mindset of creation and ideation to accommodate the remote worker, the office worker and all that comes in between.

The need to create jobs across all sectors is key to growth, prosperity and the well-being of society. Our universities collaborate closely with industry, government and agencies to meet the educational skill shortages worldwide and they conduct regular research and reviews to enhance and improve graduate employability and readiness for employment.

Employability

The nature and place of work is rapidly changing. Jobs of the future are unknown, and the advanced use of artificial intelligence and machine learning demands that graduates are adaptable global workers who are prepared to upskill/reskill to meet changing world needs. Universities are constantly seeking ways to improve the professional quality and employability of their graduates, emphasizing the development of higher-level skills through a broad curriculum.

There is little doubt that certain skills will become more in demand in the future with more reliance in areas such as Big Data and Artificial Intelligence. However, the growing world population will continue to require human intervention in dealing with human nutrition and health, education, climate change, entrepreneurship and business, science, environmental science, engineering, mathematics, agriculture, animal welfare, law, languages and the social sciences.

Employers are looking for flexible and adaptable mindsets in graduates and a high level of interpersonal communication skills to deal with changing world demands. Attitude and aptitude set the graduate apart from the crowd. Graduates will be expected to work in a hybrid manner across land and time borders, working remotely, semi-remotely or at the office, regardless of domicile. The graduate of the future will be nomadic and agile, driven by connectivity to the world.

Entrepreneurial spirit

Great entrepreneurs have passion, curiosity and ambition. They learn from the mistakes of other entrepreneurs and understand that to become successful comes with great personal sacrifice. The world of entrepreneurship is a 24/7 endeavour as you are responsible for every aspect of the business. There is little room for work–life balance particularly in the early years. Family and friends need to understand the sacrifice that has to be made. Many but not all entrepreneurs are successful. It is the passion and ambition that keeps the entrepreneur focused as problems are tackled and navigated to achieve ambitious goals.

The entrepreneur needs to be a good networker, communicate well, make best use of time and think strategically to develop the business into the future by adapting to consumer preferences, evolving markets and global demand.

Successful entrepreneurs exist because of their inner drive and ambition and their ability to stay the course when things get tough. They need to be constantly listening, learning and adapting and have the courage to take calculated risks. If you are planning to set up your own business, get in touch with the university services, who will be able to direct you appropriately in your research before starting your journey. Many universities offer modules across courses on entrepreneurship which students find most beneficial during their university years and beyond.

Universities encourage and foster a culture of entrepreneurship through 'incubators' and other facilities. This is evident in the many business-related societies enjoyed by students. These societies invite high-profile guest speakers and alumni, facilitate competitions and skills workshops and provide students with the perfect practical introduction to good business practice.

Intrapreneurial spirit

We give much attention to developing the entrepreneurial spirit at university and in our wider society. However, we must not ignore the 'intrapreneurial' spirit which determines the success of the organization.

The 'intrapreneur' thinks and acts with a business owner's head within an organization. This thinking promotes growth and development, greater opportunity and motivation of employees who are afforded a chance to flourish and bring new ideas for efficiencies and effectiveness in an open work culture.

The value of a university education

One of the ways the value of a university education can be determined is through robust assessment defining standards across particular disciplines, giving employers quality assurance regarding academic achievements. In the course of a typical university education over three or four years, students develop an invaluable set of skills, including:

- a deep sense of enquiry
- an ability to ask the right questions
- a strong broad base of knowledge in the discipline they study
- a range of intellectual skills that develop their mental abilities
- critical thinking skills
- how to analyse and sort data
- how to solve problems
- how to extend what they learn and to generate new ideas and concepts
- how to deal with knowledge in a critical and analytical way
- how to communicate information and argument in a well-reasoned manner
- thinking 'outside the box'

There is little doubt that a university education leads to a better standard of living and a greater social network. It also facilitates an ability to earn additional lifetime income giving a key understanding of the acquisition and business of knowledge and the place and value of continuous professional development and lifelong learning.

Postgraduate study

Studying at postgraduate level is demanding. There is no right or wrong time to take on this study, but it must be the right time for you, and more importantly happen at the right time in your life.

Some questions to ask:

- Why am I following this line of study?
- Where do I see it bringing me on my career path on completion?
- Can I afford it?
- Who will it impact on?

You can study part-time or full-time, which works well at master's level. However, taking on part-time study at PhD level will take over your life for many years given that the full-time course of study at this level takes between three and four years to complete and part-time around six years. If this is the avenue you wish to pursue, you must think carefully why you want to do it, what your end goal may be, what university you will attend and who is going to supervise you over the time of this study.

Only you are best placed to make that decision, which will rest on many issues – these are elaborated on later in this section.

Finance plays a major part in this decision and most students are already overburdened with student loans on completion of their undergraduate studies and need to start earning as a matter of necessity rather than choice.

Some students, for example those with computer science degrees and business combination degrees, can sometimes find work more easily than other graduates once their academic grades are achieved and references are in order. In such cases, graduates can pursue part-time postgraduate study which can fit around their work commitments and still offer the opportunity of earning as you learn.

On the other hand, some graduates will need to conduct further study in order to professionalize before they can begin work. For example, this could be typical of graduates with law or psychology degrees.

Your choice of supervisor at PhD level is crucial. In the first instance, you need to establish if he or she is expert in the field and if there is scope for your enquiry. You must establish whether this enquiry has potential for study at PhD level. In science fields there are many funding opportunities available which need to be explored.

Your choice is dependent on so many different influencing factors in your life and your future plans, your finances and your personal situation.

- What other commitments have you in life, for example?
- Have you a partner and/or a family or other personal commitments that would interfere with your ability to work very long hours, days, weeks and months and cope with rejection along the way?
- Is there funding available by way of scholarship or grant?
- Is this funding sufficient to meet your needs over three to four years?

You will need to be self-motivated and resilient for such commitment. Once again, you will have to be able to accept being at the bottom of the ladder after being so close to the top with your last academic achievement. You will need to conduct extensive background research into how your supervisor works and engages with students and how you see these types of arrangements fitting in with your life and your personality type. The supervisor–student relationship is a long and often bumpy road so there is no time for personality clashes.

While most employers do not seek out graduates with PhDs, if you wish to pursue a career in academia or in research, then a PhD is an essential part of your toolkit. This qualification, along with an active appetite for research, is seen as fundamental in order to acquire a lecturing position in any higher education institution today. These institutions look for the brightest and the best to lead graduates in different disciplines to fulfil economic and societal obligation.

Lifelong learning

The rapid growth of globalization and automation together with climate change and consumer preferences dictate an unpredictable future, a future where the focus has to be on the adaptability and flexibility of the modern worker. An appetite for learning is essential and the ability to source and assimilate credible information will remain a significant challenge into the future.

Through your university education you will become responsible for your own learning and acquire the art of 'learning how to learn'. You will experience leadership in an environment which fosters an appreciation of the value of lifelong learning and its place in the growth and development of our world across all sectors. Change is inevitable and we need to become drivers in managing our own destinies on this journey.

Engagement with constant learning helps us to understand change and how to live and act in the changing world around us. As our roles and interests evolve, we need to bridge many boundaries to cope with these changes. Reflection on experiences feeds into our need for further learning, which when introduced at the right time becomes highly motivational and insightful.

A healthy and positive attitude towards change and to continued learning facilitates mobility and employability which are essential components of the toolkit required to meet the needs of our contemporary world.

The gig economy

In our contemporary world, workers like to choose where and when they work and how to create new opportunities. The growth and development of the 'gig' economy emerged from the global recession of 2008, transforming the traditional nature of work. In essence the gig economy refers to freelancing or contract work. Working where and when you could to make ends meet was its driver, evoking creative working arrangements comprising freelancing, contract, part-time and agency work. We can all identify with the gig economy workers in our goods delivery and transportation industries where there is no long-term commitment from either workers or organizations.

In many cases this freelancing work arrangement leads to significant benefits and rewards. While this type of work is most beneficial to the organization it can also afford the successful individual flexibility through the variety of work and autonomy within projects. On the other hand, the work offers no benefits, can be a lonely journey, and payment of taxes generally rests with the gig worker. Banks do not look favourably on lending to gig workers due to the erratic nature of their income, which can negatively affect the social fabric of family and society.

The division of labour is constantly changing largely due to the higher level of automation and the development of technology leading to more efficient ways of production through machines and algorithms for today's life tasks.

Historically automation has shifted the focus of workers and tasks, and while the advent of the digital age may pose a threat to jobs in some sectors, there will be a greater need for human intervention to solve problems, to shape and share knowledge and to influence.

Global connectivity

The onset of digitalization has expedited the immediacy of the creation of a world where information and communication channels keep us constantly connected and challenged.

Global connectivity is vital for our world to function and is challenged by disruption, be that by design or by nature. Over centuries we have seen the effects of war, recession, natural disasters, pandemics and continued social and political unrest. The consequences are evident in commerce and supply chains, shocked economies, mass unemployment, poorer living conditions and an increase in mental health issues.

Global connectivity facilitates learning different skills, learning from different cultures, about how other cultures can bring different solutions to problems. The more we learn from a diversity of populations and their cultures, the better we can deal with current and emerging global challenges. These interactions force us to think more broadly, approaching problems from different perspectives, thinking laterally in non-traditional ways.

In our world we can see how connected we have become with the biggest single machine constructed by humanity, the Internet. Through this medium, information flows everywhere, regardless of time zones or geographical borders. The evidence of multiple countries' engagement in the design of machinery and smart technologies, from ideation to innovation and creation, from design to assembly, creates an interdependent and interconnected global supply chain. The rewards of the sharing of medical science discovery can be enjoyed across continents in real time, serving multiple nations. The advancement of cheaper smartphones has changed the way we live forever, influencing how we communicate and disseminate information. Social media shapes our world culture, business, politics and much more.

At university you will engage with diversity across people, cultures and mindsets. Working in multicultural teams will challenge your thinking to prepare you for future work challenges and how you can apply theoretical models to practice. Countries are unable to work in isolation and the graduates of the future will need to be prepared to work in the wider connected world rather than in their local or regionalized spaces.

The ideal graduate will possess the defined skills and knowledge of their particular area of study, but above all they will need to be able to hit the ground running as rounded individuals with an ability to think outside the box, to be useful in professional practice as quickly as possible, to problem-solve, to communicate in a fast-moving digital age, to meet the needs of an unpredictable society, to be intrapreneurial and/or entrepreneurial, to be flexible and adaptable and to cope with change, to be mobile and employable but most importantly to be contributing citizens to our evolving world.

In the UK a post-study work visa allows international students to work or look for work in the UK for up to two years after graduation. However, British graduates may face challenges acquiring visas to work overseas. Check this out with the international office at your university who may be able to assist you.

Concluding paragraphs

Mobility, employability and active citizenship are key to your success and contribution to the world we live in. It is in this context that we need to understand that you are being educated for a world of change, that jobs for life are things of the past and much of the future depends on creativity, innovation, entrepreneurship and intrapreneurship.

Given the unpredictable nature of the workplace today, it is difficult to foresee many of the jobs of the future. Follow your own dream. Therein lies the key to your opportunities. Embrace every learning opportunity and every service that can enhance that opportunity.

Regardless of your involvement in sport and community activity, seek to develop your talents and interests. Widen your circle by joining clubs and societies at university.

Get to know what you are good at and identify what you need help with. If you have a natural flair for languages, work on them as they are key to mobility and employability worldwide. Where support centres run specific courses or drop-in clinics to assist with any of your subjects, make the most of them.

Build your own set of unique skills and try to do something new every semester, or at least every academic year. Keep this practice with you for life, whether learning to cook, paint or take photographs. It's good for the soul.

Develop your network and get to know the university campus and the university systems. Understand the importance of the gatekeepers of the university, the administrative staff who liaise with the academics, those who take in assignments, those who can give you access to study rooms and those who hold the keys to buildings.

Be prepared to work hard at getting the best out of group and team situations. Be prepared, visible and vocal at tutorials. Be clever in your approach to study and if you have part-time work, make it work for you, not the other way round.

Fitness and diet are all-important. Make your home a calm and stress-free place.

Be kind to others. You will reap the reward many times over, maybe not today or tomorrow but in time to come. Take ownership and responsibility for all that you do. It is your future; it is your destiny; it is all yours. There will be tough times ahead but remember that there is always help and support available.

Don't look back – tomorrow is always a new day.

Make it a good one.

Troubleshooting section

Top tips

- All CVs, covering letters and application forms should be tailored to specific jobs
- Seek out a mock interview – it works
- Check out your social networking profiles
- Be careful about the content you post on social media
- Make a list of all your contacts and update it regularly
- Make time to work on your career development and be consistent about doing this
- Take up a new interest every year

This could be you

I feel under pressure to study for a master's/PhD but I'm not sure it is right for me
Take time to consider the pros and cons for such a decision. What is your purpose? What's in it for you? Can you afford it? Are you clear in your goals? Seek out help from your tutor and the careers advisory service.

I am applying for jobs but don't seem to be having any success in getting called for interviews
Maybe you are not exploring enough avenues. Algorithms are used by employers to reach suitable candidates. Are you tailoring your CV to the competencies specified in the job description?

Have you looked at your social media presence and how you have positioned your profile, and has it been updated?

It is vital to tailor covering letters, introductions, applications and CVs to the role, tasks and competencies which are detailed in the job specification. It is also equally important to ensure that your layout is user-friendly, relevant and free from errors – which are also picked up by those nasty algorithms! Seek some advice from the careers advisory service.

International students

I am concerned about applying for jobs, further study and visa issues

Before embarking on any further study or job searching, always establish your visa requirements relating to work or further study, as the rules vary considerably depending on your country of origin and residency. Check this out with the careers advisory service and the international office at your university, who will be able to direct you appropriately to clarify your situation.

If you are considering postgraduate study as an international student, your status will attract higher fees in England. It is important to understand your financial situation fully before you commit to further study. Check out if there are any extended visa benefits to be gained from this study.

Building employability skills

- You will need to work on your presentation, communication and team-working skills which are considered critical elements of your toolkit in seeking any kind of work. Employers like their workforce to be adaptable and flexible and will need to see these skills demonstrated at interview.
- The interview is centred around your story and how you sell it. This is a process which takes time to perfect. Seek support from a competent career development professional or careers advisory service. Early intervention will pay dividends in the long run.

Selected Reading

Aiken, M. (2016) *The Cyber Effect: A Pioneering Cyberpsychologist Explains How Human Behavior Changes Online*. London: John Murray.

Allan, G. (2014) *Working with Substance Users: A Guide to Effective Interventions*. Basingstoke: Palgrave Macmillan.

Arday, J. and Mirza, H.S. (eds) (2018) *Dismantling Race in Higher Education: Racism, Whiteness and Decolonising the Academy*. Basingstoke: Palgrave Macmillan.

Blumberg, B., Cooper, D. and Schindler, P. (2014) *Business Research Methods*, 4th edn. Maidenhead: McGraw-Hill Education.

Bordens, K.S. and Abbott, B.B. (2018) *Research Design and Methods: A Process Approach*, 10th edn. Maidenhead: McGraw-Hill Education.

Burchard, B. (2017) *High Performance Habits: How Extraordinary People Become that Way*. Carlsbad, CA: Hay House.

Collins COBUILD Dictionary (2018) *Collins COBUILD Advanced Learner's Dictionary: The Source of Authentic English*, Collins COBUILD Dictionaries for Learners, 9th edn. Glasgow: Harper Collins.

Criado Perez, C. (2019) *Invisible Women: Exposing Data Bias in a World Designed for Men*. London: Chatto & Windus.

Davey, G. (2018) *The Anxiety Epidemic: The Causes of Our Modern-Day Anxieties*. London: Little, Brown.

Denscombe, M. (2012) *Research Proposals: A Practical Guide*. Maidenhead: Open University Press/McGraw-Hill Education.

Duhigg, C. (2013) *The Power of Habit: Why We Do What We Do and How to Change*. London: Random House.

Dweck, C.S. (2008) *Mindset: The New Psychology of Success*. New York: Random House.

Eberhardt, J. (2019) *Biased: The New Science of Race and Inequality*. London: William Heinemann.

Field, A. (2009) *Discovering Statistics Using SPSS: And Sex and Drugs and Rock'n'Roll*. London: Sage.

Ford, M. (2018) *Architects of Intelligence: The Truth about AI from the People Building It*. Birmingham: Packt Publishing Ltd.

Goleman, D. (2009) *Emotional Intelligence: Why It Can Matter More than IQ*. London: Bloomsbury.

Hawking, S. (2018) *Brief Answers to the Big Questions*. London: John Murray.

Katzenbach, J.R. and Smith, D.K. (2015) *The Wisdom of Teams: Creating the High-Performance Organization*. Boston, MA: Harvard Business School Publishing.

Levit, A. (2019) *Humanity Works: Merging Technologies and People for the Workforce of the Future*. London: Kogan Page.

Levitin, D. (2014) *The Organized Mind: Thinking Straight in the Age of Information Overload*. London: Penguin Random House.

Lewis, R.D. (2018) *When Cultures Collide: Leading Across Cultures*, 4th edn. London: Nicholas Brealey Publishing.

Marquet, L. David (2019) *Turn the Ship Around!: A True Story of Turning Followers into Leaders*. London: Penguin Random House.

Marshall, T. (2018) *Divided: Why We're Living in an Age of Walls*. London: Elliott and Thompson.

McChrystal, General S., Collins, T., Silverman, D. and Fussell, C. (2015) *Team of Teams: New Rules of Engagement for a Complex World*. London: Penguin.

Mewburn, I., Firth, K. and Lehmann, S. (2018) *How to Fix Your Academic Writing Trouble: A Practical Guide*. Maidenhead: McGraw-Hill Education.

Murray, N. and Hughes, G. (2008) *Writing up Your University Assignments and Research Projects*. Maidenhead: McGraw-Hill Education/Open University Press.

O'Connor, C. (2013) *Cracking the College Code: A Practical Guide to Making the Most of the First Year College Experience*. Dublin: C.J. Fallon.

O'Mara, S. (2019) *In Praise of Walking: The New Science of How We Walk and Why It's Good for Us*. London: Bodley Head.

Oxford English Dictionary (2010) *Oxford Dictionary of English*, 3rd edn. Oxford: Oxford University Press.

Peters, S. (2012) *The Chimp Paradox: The Mind Management Programme for Confidence, Success and Happiness*. London: Ebury Publishing.

Ritter, R.M. (ed.) (2016) *New Oxford Style Manual: The World's Most Trusted Reference Books*, 3rd edn. Oxford: Oxford University Press.

Sinclair, C. (2010) *Grammar: A Friendly Approach*, 2nd edn. Maidenhead: McGraw-Hill Education/Open University Press.

Sire, J.W. (2015) *Naming the Elephant: Worldview as a Concept*, 2nd edn. Downers Grove, IL: Inter Varsity Press.

Sumpter, D. (2018) *Outnumbered: From Facebook and Google to Fake News and Filter-Bubbles – the Algorithms that Control Our Lives*. London: Bloomsbury Sigma.

Susskind, J. (2018) *Future Politics: Living Together in a World Transformed by Tech*. Oxford: Oxford University Press.

Talbot, C. (2015) *Studying at a Distance: A Guide for Students*, 4th edn. Maidenhead: McGraw-Hill Education/Open University Press.

Thomlinson, N. (2016) *Race, Ethnicity and the Women's Movement in England, 1968–1993*, Palgrave Studies in the History of Social Movements. Basingstoke: Palgrave Macmillan.

Trompenaars, F. and Hampden-Turner, C. (2020) *Riding the Waves of Culture: Understanding Diversity in Global Business*, 4th edn. New York: McGraw-Hill.

Waite, M. (ed.) (2009) *Oxford Thesaurus of English*. Oxford: Oxford University Press.

West, D.M. (2019) *The Future of Work: Robots, AI, and Automation*. Washington, DC: The Brookings Institution.

Useful Links and Resources

Student finance

Student loans: www.gov.uk/student-finance-register-login
Money Saving Expert: www.moneysavingexpert.com/
The Money Advice Service: www.moneyadviceservice.org.uk/en/categories/student-and-graduate-money
Citizens Advice: www.citizensadvice.org.uk/
WiseBread.com: www.wisebread.com/

International students

UK Council for International Student Affairs (UKCISA): www.ukcisa.org.uk/
British Council: www.britishcouncil.org/
Visa information: www.gov.uk/student-visa

Student organizations and leisure

National Union of Students: www.nus.org.uk/
RAISE: www.raise-network.com/home/
Internships, placements and graduate jobs: www.milkround.com/

Leisure

Time Out: www.timeout.com/london
Ticketmaster: www.ticketmaster.co.uk/
The List: www.list.co.uk
The Sunday Times Culture: www.thetimes.co.uk/arts-culture
Exploring More of the UK: exploringmore.co.uk/
Visit England: www.visitengland.com/
The British Museum: www.britishmuseum.org/

Shopping

Books: www.amazon.co.uk/; http://thebookpond.com/
General: www.ebay.co.uk/; www.amazon.co.uk/
Fashion: www.depop.com/; www.asos.com/

Groceries: www.asda.com/; www.tesco.com/; www.sainsburys.co.uk/
Discount codes: www.groupon.co.uk/discount-codes/ebay; www.myunidays.com/GB/en-GB

Student health

Student Health: www.studenthealth.co.uk/
NHS Student Health: www.nhs.uk/live-well/healthy-body/getting-medical-care-as-a-student/; www.nhs.uk/apps-library/student-health-app/
Drink Aware: www.drinkaware.co.uk/
My Mind Health: https://mymindhealth.com/
Student Minds: www.studentminds.org.uk/
Heads Together: www.headstogether.org.uk/
Give Us a Shout: https://giveusashout.org/
Mental Health: www.mentalhealth.org.uk/
Head Talks: www.headtalks.com/
The Calm Zone: www.thecalmzone.net/
The Samaritans: www.samaritans.org/

Student welfare

Student recipes: www.studentrecipes.com
Recipepuppy.com: www.recipepuppy.com/
The Uni Guide: www.theuniguide.co.uk/
The Federation of Student Islamic Societies: www.fosis.org.uk/
Union of Jewish Students: www.ujs.org.uk/
The Christian Unions: www.uccf.org.uk/
Jobs and careers: www.prospects.ac.uk/

Student learning

The Teaching Excellence and Student Outcomes Framework: www.officeforstudents.org.uk/advice-and-guidance/teaching/about-the-tef/
The world's largest collection of open access research papers: https://core.ac.uk/
Kahn academy: www.khanacademy.org/
Ted talks: www.ted.com
YouTube: www.youtube.com/
Free learning resources: www.coursera.org/
The Quality Assurance Agency for Higher Education: www.qaa.ac.uk
Future Learn (study skills): www.futurelearn.com/subjects/study-skills-courses

General information about universities

The Complete University Guide: www.thecompleteuniversityguide.co.uk/
Student Times: www.studenttimes.org/
TopUniversities.com: www.topuniversities.com/
Office for students: www.officeforstudents.org.uk/
Office of the Independent Adjudicator for Higher Education: www.oiahe.org.uk/
UCAS–The Universities and Colleges Admissions Service: www.ucas.com
Discover university: https://discoveruni.gov.uk/

Index

Page numbers with 't' are tables.

abroad
   travelling and studying 86–7
   volunteering 108
   working and work placements 19, 109, 126
absences 32–3
academic activities 36–45
academic difficulties 15, 29–30
academic integrity 44–5
academic services 48, 54
academic writing 13, 43–4, 67–71
   see also essay writing
academic year 27–8
accommodation 6–9, 48
   at home 5–6
   second year 105
   studying abroad 86–7
acknowledging sources 39, 44, 74–5
action plans, and goal setting 58
action words 117, 117t
advisors, academic 34
alcohol 100
alumni body 115
analytical thinking 62–3
anxiety 54, 99–100, 102
   and examinations 73
apostrophes 71
application forms 116–17, 116t, 117t
applying for work 114–15, 127
assault, sexual 85–6
assessment 28, 72–4
   continuous 42, 45, 46
   second year 104
assessments, and graduate schemes 113
assignments 30, 42
attendance 32–3
   lectures 38, 54

backing up work 42, 52, 64
belief, self- 15, 52, 57, 79, 80
budgeting 6, 9, 16, 17–19, 106

care leavers 50–1
careers 16
   and the future of work 120
   services 49, 107, 112
chaplaincy services 49
class representatives 13, 35
cleaning 7, 9
clubs 5, 8, 105–6
commitment, lack of 15
communication
   and culture 84
   interpersonal 97–8, 102
   skills 76–80
   with the university 33–4
   see also language
community life 8, 15–16
confidence, and presentations 79, 80
connectivity, global 125–6
consent, sexual 85–6
cooking and diet 8–9, 18, 88, 89–90
counselling services 49–50, 99, 100
course, choice of wrong 14, 24
coursework 42–3, 45, 46
covering letters, for job applications 117
Covid-19 106, 112
credits 29
criminal records 100
critical thinking 12–13, 62–3
culture and diversity 84–5
CVs 110, 112, 116, 117, 119

deadlines 30, 32, 38, 42, 53
demonstrations 41
diet 8–9, 18, 88, 89–90
disability services 50
diversity 10, 84–5
division of labour 124
drafting stage of academic writing 69–70
drugs 100

editing stage of academic writing 70–1
electronic systems 39–40
email 33, 116
emotional well-being 94–5
employability 25, 60, 120–1
employment, graduate 110
engage 52
enrolment 36
entrepreneurs 121
Equality Act 85
Equality and Human Rights Commission 85
essay writing 72
examinations 28, 30, 42–3, 45
  and enrolment 36
  and fear 73–4
examiners 13
exercising 90–1
expectations 2, 17

failure, examination 73–4
fears 2, 4, 73, 81, 94
  see also anxiety
feedback, and lecturers 81
fees 12, 36
finance
  budgeting 9, 18–19
  and mature students 21
  and postgraduate study 123
  resources 131
  and work placements 109
  worries 16, 49
fitting in 55
formatting stage of academic writing 71
fourth year *see* third year/fourth year
freelancing work 124–5
'Freshers' week' 26–7
friends 4, 7, 105–6
future of work 120

gap year 113–14
gender, and identity 85
gig economy 124–5
global connectivity 125–6
goal setting 57–8, 89
  and emotional well-being 95
  and interpersonal communication 98
  and mental well-being 93
  and physical well-being 92
  and spiritual well-being 97

grading 15, 45, 46t
graduate schemes 113
grants 16, 18, 123
group work 43, 61–2, 84
guest speakers 41

habit 60
handbooks 19, 30–2, 52, 104
health services 50, 94, 100, 131
help, seeking 15, 47–52, 101, 102
home, living at 5–6
homesickness 8, 55

identity 83, 85, 110
illness, and absences 32
independent learning 12–13, 62–3
induction/orientation 3, 37
international students 24–5, 84
  and academic writing 44
  and accommodation 7
  and attendance 32
  cultural issues 6
  employment rights 19
  fitting in 55
  and health services 50
  homesickness 55
  language 4, 24, 82
  resources 131
  and studying 82
  visas after graduation 126, 128
  well-being 102
Internet 125
internships 107–8, 113
interpersonal communication 97–8, 102
interviews, job 117–19
intrapreneurs 121–2

job fairs 112, 115

laboratories 41
language 17
  and culture 84
  and international students 4, 24, 82
  and studying abroad 87
  and work placements 109
learning centres 51
learning objectives/outcomes 28, 29
lecturers 9, 11t, 33, 38, 39, 40, 44
  and feedback 81
  help from 15, 35

Index

and the second year 104
lectures 29, 38, 52
   attendance 13
   and listening skills 66
   note-taking 63–4
   preparation for 63
libraries 39
life skills 8–9
lifelong learning 124
listening skills 66
loans 16, 18, 24
location, accommodation 7
Loci (place) method 65
looking for work 114-20, 116t, 117t

mature students 14, 20–1
meditation 96
memory, and studying 64–5
mental health 14, 49–50, 101
   see also well-being
mentoring/personal tutoring services 51–2, 81
method, giving presentations 78–9
modules 37–8
motivation, lack of 17

networking 4, 41, 55, 107, 115
note-taking 63–4, 75
notes, giving presentations 79

online
   interviews 118
   learning 21, 75–6
orientation 3, 37

parents, and universities 12, 23
participation 41, 52, 62, 104
physical well-being 89–92
placements, work 106, 107, 109–10
plagiarism 44, 74–5
planning stage of academic writing 68–9
portfolios 42
postgraduate study 122–4, 127
PowerPoint 77
practicals 41
practice, giving presentations 79–80
presentations 41, 76–80
proofreading 71
psychometric testing 113
public transport 7, 18

questioning style, interview 118

reading, as a skill 42
reading lists 39
reading weeks 43
recruitment events 112
referencing academic work 39, 44, 74–5
registration/enrolment 36
rejection, and job hunting 119–20, 127
relationships
   parent and student 12
   student and university 11–12, 11t, 23
remote/distance learning 21
rental agreements 7, 87
research 9–10, 41–2, 66–7
   when looking for work 115–16
resilience 100–1
resources 131
responsibility 12, 15, 25, 52
   and academic challenges 29
   taking 3
rewards, and goal setting 89
risk assessments 87
Roman Room system 65
rules and regulations 30–2, 53

salaries 113
school systems, and university systems 10–13, 11t
second year 103–10
self, and well-being 87–8
self-confidence 79, 80
self-employment 120
self-management 3, 4, 52
semesters 27
seminars and tutorials 10, 40–1
setting goals 57–8, 89
sexual consent 85–6
sexuality 85
sleep 88–9, 102
social development 2, 3–5, 104–5
social difficulties 15–16
social media 33, 115
societies 5, 8, 105–6, 131
spellcheck errors 116t
spiritual well-being 96–7
STEM subjects 17
student advisory systems 51–2
student services 17, 35, 52, 94, 99
Students' Unions 5, 8, 17

class reps 35
and enrolment 36
and 'Freshers' week' 27
and getting help 50
and unfair disadvantage 85
study groups 61–2
studying
   abroad 86–7
   planning 88–9
   for results 57
   skills 64–5
   time 46–7
subject matter, and presentations 78
substance use and abuse 100
suicide 99
support centres 51
support services 17, 47–52
systems, universities and schools 10–13, 11t

teaching methods/delivery 28
team working and learning 60–1, 102
terminology 12, 44, 54
terms 28
third year/fourth year 110–11
   applying for work 114–20
   gap year 113–14
   graduate schemes 113
   internships 113
   job fairs 112, 115
   university resources 112
time-management 12, 58–60

Time-wasting challenge exercise 59
toolkits 19–20
travelling abroad 86–7
tutorials/seminars 10, 40–1
tutoring system 13–14, 34–5, 52, 54
   and career advice 113
   tutorials 13
   see also mentoring
typing 52

under-preparedness in subject areas 17
underperformance, and team working 61

vacation time 19, 22, 107
value, of a university education 122–3
volunteering 108

well-being 87–8
   emotional 94–5
   mental 92–4
   physical 89–92
   spiritual 96–7
withdrawal from courses 14–17
work, looking for 114–20, 116t, 117t
work ethic 52
work placements 109–10
working while studying 19, 21–2, 106–7
workshops 15, 41, 61, 81, 82, 99
workload 12, 21, 47, 61, 104, 106
writer's block 68
writing, academic 13, 43–4, 67–71